PORSCHE BOXSTER & CAYMAN

ULTIMATE OWNERS' GUIDE

Porsche Boxster & Cayman

Mark Bennett
PMM Books

PORSCHE BOXSTER & CAYMAN

All rights reserved. No part of this publication may be reproduced, copied, stored on a retrieval system or transmitted in any form or by any means, electronic, mechanical, photocopy, recording or otherwise without prior written permission from the publisher.

The information presented here represents the best available to the author at the time of going to press. The book is intended as a guide only. The author, the publisher or the associated companies can accept no liabilities for any material loss resulting from the use of this information.

This book uses model-names, type numbers and terms that are the property of the trademark holders and are used here for identification only. Several specialists or specific brands are mentioned throughout the book. These are products and services that have only been spoken of positively by the experts who have contributed to this book. These specialists have made no commercial endorsement to the author or publisher.

This is an independent publication.
There is no association with Porsche SE or any of its subsidiaries.
The name of Porsche is used only for identification purposes.

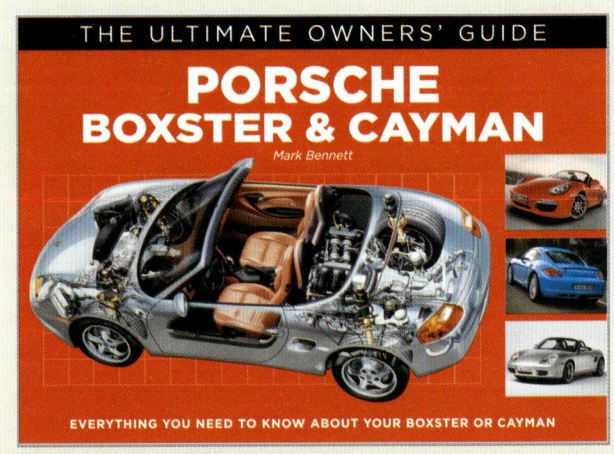

Copyright: Mark Bennett 2010

First published 2010.   ISBN 978 1 906712 01 3

Reprinted 2011

Design & Layout: SD Design

Photo credits: Mark Bennett, Porsche archive

Printed and bound in India by Replika Press Pvt. Ltd.

Published by PMM Books, an imprint of Peter Morgan Media Ltd., PO Box 2561, Marlborough, Wiltshire, SN8 1YD, Great Britain.
Telephone: +44 1672 514038   E-mail: sales@pmmbooks.com   Website: www.pmmbooks.com

2 Ultimate Owners' Guide

CONTENTS

4	Introduction	44	Bodyshell care	134	Wheels and tyres
6	Story of the Boxster	72	Maintenance schedules	143	Cooling and heating
12	Key development milestones	92	Engine	147	Electrical system
16	Special models	111	Transmission	170	Trackday preparation
22	Knowing your car	115	Suspension and steering	174	Acknowledgements
36	Emergencies	122	Brakes	175	Index

Ultimate Owners' Guide

INTRODUCTION

Many things may have first drawn you to the Porsche Boxster or Cayman.

Maybe it was the beautiful lines of the car, the performance, the handling, the mid-engined balance, or simply that Porsche badge. Whatever it was that appealed to you when you first bought the car, by now you will surely have found there are many other excellent characteristics that have become apparent.

My journey into Porsche ownership started with a 10 year old 944, which looked and drove like new. It was a revelation after my previous car – a Bertone-FIAT X1/9 VS that I bought new and in just 8 years returned to the original compounds from which it was made – it simply rusted away! The Porsche's quality shone through and despite it being out of production for a few years already, I was often asked if it was a new car. That same experience has happened to me again with my Boxster S – only more so.

A good Boxster or Cayman will be a pleasure to drive, has great performance and superb looks. It can easily be used for a touring holiday by 2 people, while doing the occasional track-day along the way (I know – my partner and I have enjoyed 2 week tours around Europe, taking in France, then top down in the Swiss, Italian, and Austrian Alps followed by 150mph on Germany's derestricted Autobahns and finishing off with a day at the Nürburgring Nordschleife).

This is such a versatile and practical car! I'd almost say it was perfect.

But however perfect any car is, there are always likely to be things you wish you knew more about, the little things that make it easier to live with, or some easy maintenance that can be done yourself. I have owned my Boxster S for some 9 years and I have become the Boxster Register Secretary of the Porsche Club Great Britain.

This book isn't intended to be a workshop manual. Nor does it cover complex or difficult mechanical procedures, nor DIY servicing. Rather, it is a guide to tasks that most owners can accomplish without damaging the car, or more importantly, themselves.

The idea is to cover a variety of tasks that are quite common that owners might need to do from time to time.

Servicing is not covered as most owners do not have access to the Porsche electronic service tool PST2. The PST2 electronics interrogation tool is essential during the servicing of the car to check for faults, and sometimes, to reset certain parameters or fault codes.

As always, do not attempt anything if you are in any way unsure that you can complete the task safely and completely.

But driving it is what it is really all about and I hope you get as much enjoyment from your car as I have from mine.

Mark Bennett
Farnborough, England

THE STORY OF THE BOXSTER

The story of how the Boxster appeared in the showrooms is one based in turbulent times for Porsche. In the early 1990s, the Stuttgart-based sports car manufacturer had been hit hard by the combined blows of worldwide economic recession and greatly increased Pacific rim competition in its key export market – the USA. This was at a time when its own product line was seen as largely obsolete. The result was a massive slump in sales that took the company to the edge of bankruptcy.

Porsche had a model range that was made up of three models – the V8 928, the 4-cylinder 944 and the classic air-cooled 6-cylinder 911.

The 928 had once been intended to replace the evergreen 911 and steady development over some 15 years had produced an excellent car that was a world leader in many respects. Nevertheless, it had failed to replace the 911 in the hearts of the Porsche buying public, being considered more of a grand tourer than a nimble sports car.

The 944 suffered from being regarded as too expensive for a 4-cylinder car and it didn't have enough performance for the price point at which it was being sold. From late 1991, an 83% new, facelifted model went on sale, called the 968. It provided short term help but this was only a stop-gap measure.

Finally, the 911 model of the time - the 964 – had reached its development limits. The classic rear-engined sports car had been in production for some 30 years and this evolution process had resulted in a labour intensive and

Above: The 944 was seen as expensive for a 4-cylinder car by the 1990s. Below: 964 - by 1993 this was a 30 year old design

Ultimate Owners' Guide

Giancarlo Baghetti in the 1963 Targa Florio. There is no mistaking the heritage of the Boxster in the lines of his Spyder

expensive assembly process that used outdated production lines and methods. Ever stricter environmental and safety regulations meant the 911 also lacked the passive safety features that would soon be required by markets around the world. The classic air-cooled 6-cylinder engine was struggling to meet new exhaust emissions requirements and with none of the sound deadening effect that conventional water cooling would have, the old air-cooled design was often too loud to meet strict noise requirements.

Given this ageing product line, it was no surprise that sales began to slide downwards.

Something had to change or Porsche would not be in business much longer.

Almost inevitably, this period also coincided with a turbulent time at the top of the company. Chief Executive Officer Arno Bohn had taken the Porsche reins in March 1990, but there was soon conflict within the supervisory board about his suitability. After several key personnel had departed over the next year or so, Bohn departed in September 1992. The supervisory board nominated Dr Wendelin Wiedeking, a production engineer who had been with the company for several

The 911 struggled to meet new noise regulations

The 968 was 83% new and bought much needed time

years, to replace him.

Although Wiedeking had been a key part in an upgrade of facilities during the late '80's, he also knew that a whole new approach to manufacturing the cars would be needed for Porsche to become competitive again and that a new product range would be required to take advantage of these new methods.

Luckily a new variant of the 911 (the 993) had just finished development and it would go in to production as the last of the air-cooled 911 range. This, together with the facelifted 944 – the 968 – would buy much needed time to develop the new production methods and cars.

Toyota were approached for assistance in developing 'just in time' production methods, and the Zuffenhausen plant in Stuttgart was redeveloped around these concepts.

The new models would start with a new 2 seat roadster model called type 986, this would become known as the 'Boxster' and alongside this the new 911 variant (the 996) would be developed.

In the late 1980s, the head of the

The Boxster concept takes shape in the Porsche design studios

Porsche styling department, Harm Lagaay, produced a concept for a 4-door car known as type 989. After much development effort, this car was cancelled before it went into production (It is alleged that at the time Dr Wiedeking reportedly commented that "a four door car does not fit in with the image of Porsche" – how times have changed!)

Although it was abandoned before production, the 989 would preview many of the styling cues of the later 986 Boxster, and even more pronounced, of the new 996 version of the 911.

In the spring of 1992 work began on the development of the type 986 Boxster and new 996. The 996 replacement design for the 993 had actually already been started some time before, but now there was a decision to share as many of the same components as possible between the two models, even though one was a 2-seat mid-engined roadster, and the other a 4-seat rear-engined coupé. (The engine placement issue being solved simply by turning the engine in the 996 around.)

PORSCHE BOXSTER & CAYMAN

In the 996, the gearbox is in front of the engine while in the Boxster it is behind the engine). Thus the 996 design was restarted from scratch to make the best use of components that could be shared between the two models – including the complete front end up to the windscreen, and the aforementioned engine design.

In January 1993, a concept model of the Boxster was shown at the Detroit Motor Show. Designed by a bright young American in Lagaay's design team, Grant Larson, the car was an instant hit. The concept car subsequently went on a world tour and received much praise from both press and public. As importantly, it brought Porsche much needed international coverage and let potential customers know that a new, more affordable model was on its way from Porsche.

The car was certainly beautiful on the outside, with exquisite interior detail touches that added to the feel that it was an expensive piece of jewellery. On the rear deck was the (now familiar) script proclaiming the upcoming model's name 'Boxster' – this being the name

In January 1993, the Boxster concept model was an immediate hit worldwide

PORSCHE BOXSTER & CAYMAN

the designers had given the new car. It was derived from the combination of 'Boxer' (for the engine configuration) and 'Roadster'. This would be the first Porsche known to all by a name, rather than a model number.

Back in Porsche's engineering centre at Weissach, near Stuttgart, the design team were working on the two new models. In the summer of 1993 the supervisory board signed off both cars for production.

That same summer saw the first of the new engines being bench tested (the concept car had no engine and had been filmed moving for promotional material by the simple method of pushing it down a slope, and past the camera…)

By 1994 Boxsters disguised as 968s were pounding around the Weissach test track. Later that year the Boxster shape was seen a little more clearly as environmental testing was carried out in the desert heat of Nevada, followed by cold weather testing in Canada.

The first pre-production models commenced manufacture in October 1995, allowing the engineers and production staff to learn how best to assemble the car and iron out any of the little assembly wrinkles that always happen with a new product.

The final production design was said to be styled after the Type 550 Spyder with which Porsche had competed at Le Mans and had won the 1956 Targa Florio outright.

To this author's eyes it also had the look of the 1960 Sebring winning RS 60 or the later 1963 W-RS Spyder.

Finally, in 1996, co-incidentally just a month after they had produced their 1,000,000th car (on July 1, 1996 – a 993 for the German Police!), Porsche launched the production version of the Boxster. August 19 1996 was the big day when production began for the first time and Boxsters started being made at Zuffenhausen in Stuttgart.

The Boxster was such a success from the very start that a year later, additional Boxster production was started by the sub-contract company Valmet at Uuisikaupunki in Finland. Valmet were specialists in providing extra production

Boxster production started on August 19, 1996

resources for manufacturers who had themselves reached capacity. Valmet made the Boxsters from components supplied by Porsche. The engines were still assembled at Porsche and then shipped to Finland. Valmet also made SAAB cars at the time and the facilities were so advanced at the plant that both Boxsters and SAABs were assembled on the same production line, with the cars intermingled. Strict production standards meant there was no difference in quality between Boxsters made in Finland and those made in Germany.

Ultimate Owners' Guide

KEY DEVELOPMENT STEPS

The Boxster started life in the now familiar guise of a 2-seat roadster, with an electrically powered folding roof, a 2.5-litre horizontally-opposed flat-6 engine and choice of 5-speed manual or automatic (Tiptronic) gearbox. From the car's introduction, the new owner has been able to specify various options from a mind-bogglingly long list.

Over its production life there has been continuous year-on-year evolutionary improvements (which are generally not big enough for Porsche to announce the result as a new model), a number of specification changes, several engine upgrades and capacity variants, the introduction of 6-speed manual gearboxes and a new type of automatic gearbox referred to as 'PDK' (short for Porsche Doppel Kupplungsgetriebe – literally meaning double clutch transmission). There have been two 'face-lifts' that have been significant enough for Porsche to advertise the car as a new, improved variant. There has also been one major redesign, known as the type 987 Boxster and a new coupé version called the Cayman.

The following is a brief introduction to the major changes that have happened through the years, which will help to identify any specific model.

Note: *Porsche model years normally start from the beginning of September the previous year, when production restarts following the regular August factory shutdown. This means that, for example, a 2001MY (Model Year) Boxster has been made between September 2000, and July 2001.*

12   Ultimate Owners' Guide

1997 Model year
Introductory model (from Aug '96)

Boxster 986
- 2.5-litre engine (2,480cc) 204bhp (150kW)
- 5-speed manual /5-speed Tiptronic gearbox
- 16-inch alloy wheels
- Options included Sport and Lux packs:

The Sport pack added leather seats, traction control, wind deflector, 17-inch wheels, 10mm lowered body, modified suspension, and uprated stabilizers. The Lux pack added leather seats, 17-inch wheels, wind deflector, air conditioning, and an on-board computer.
- Desirable options included full leather interior, climate control (air conditioning), Traction Control and sports exhaust

2000 Model year

Engine capacity increases to 2.7-litres on the Boxster. Introduction of the 3.2-litre Boxster S

Boxster 986
- 2.7-litre (2,687cc) 220bhp (161kW)
- 5-speed manual /5 speed Tiptronic gearbox
- 16-inch alloy wheels

Boxster S 986
- 3.2-litre (3,179cc) 252bhp (185kW)
- 6-speed manual /5-speed Tiptronic gearbox
- 17-inch alloy wheels, standard leather seats, roof liner, twin exhaust outlets, third radiator at centre of the front bumper, red brake callipers and titanium coloured trim.
- A full range of individually specifiable options were available for both models, including 17- and 18-inch wheels, leather trim and seats, sport suspension and Porsche Stability Management (PSM).

2003 Model year

Face-lifted model, with revised front and rear bumpers, a glass rear window replaced the previous plastic in the folding top and a glovebox.

Boxster 986
- 2.7-litre (2,687cc) 228bhp (168kW)
- 5-speed manual /5 speed Tiptronic gearbox
- 16-inch alloy wheels

Boxster S 986
- 3.2-litre (3,179cc) 260bhp (191kW)
- 6-speed manual /5 speed Tiptronic gearbox
- 17-inch wheels
- Options were similar to the 2000MY cars.

Ultimate Owners' Guide

PORSCHE BOXSTER & CAYMAN

2005 Model year	2006 Model year	2007 Model year
Major re-design of the outer bodyshell, retaining a similar overall look but revising every external panel. The interior design was given a new, harder-edged look. Power was increased, although the engine sizes remained the same. **Boxster 987** ■ 2.7-litre (2,687cc) 240bhp (176kW) ■ 5-speed manual /5-speed Tiptronic gearbox ■ 17-inch alloy wheels **Boxster S 987** ■ 3.2-litre (3,179cc) 280bhp (205kW) ■ 6-speed manual /5-speed Tiptronic gearbox ■ 18-inch alloy wheels The 6-speed manual transmission became an option on the base model Boxster. PCCB (Porsche Ceramic Composite Brake) were an expensive brake option. PSM was standard on both models. 19-inch wheels were a popular option. Sport-Chrono was available, which sharpened up the response, and together with the option of PASM Porsche Adaptive Suspension Management made for handling that could be adapted for the particular road, or indeed track, conditions.	Introduction of the Cayman S. The Cayman was designated the 987C within Porsche, indicating that it is a coupé version of the Boxster. No changes were made to the Boxsters so for brevity these have been omitted from the information for this year. **Cayman S** ■ 3.4-litre (3,387cc) 295bhp (216kW) ■ 6-speed manual /5-speed Tiptronic gearbox ■ 18-inch wheels ■ Options were as for the 2005 Model Year Boxster S.	Introduction of Cayman with 2.7-litre engine alongside 3.4-litre Cayman S. **Boxster 987** ■ 2.7-litre (2,687cc) 245bhp (180kW) ■ 5-speed manual /5-speed Tiptronic gearbox ■ 17-inch wheels **Boxster S 987** ■ 3.4-litre (3,387cc) 295bhp (216kW) ■ 6-speed manual /5-speed Tiptronic gearbox ■ 18-inch wheels ■ Options were as for the 2005 Model Year. **Cayman** ■ 2.7-litre (2,687cc) 245bhp (180kW) ■ 5-speed manual /5-speed Tiptronic gearbox ■ 17-inch wheels **Cayman S** ■ 3.4-litre (3,387cc) 295bhp (216kW) ■ 6-speed manual /5-speed Tiptronic gearbox ■ 18-inch wheels ■ Options were similar to the 2005 Model Year.

2009 Model year

Although released a little late for the particular year, with deliveries not starting until early in 2009, the Boxster and Cayman were both revised slightly externally, with major redesigns to the engines, for what would be known as the 2009 Model Year. The engine power of both Cayman models was increased to regain the small performance step lost when the Boxster gained the Cayman engines in 07. Both the base Boxster and Cayman models gained an engine size increase to 2.9-litres and a moderate power increase that made them more powerful than the original Boxster S – although simultaneously emissions were significantly reduced. A significant change was the replacement of the Tiptronic automatic gearbox by the 7-speed PDK (Porsche Doppel Kupplung) dual clutch transmission, tempting many manual owners over to the almost instantaneous gearshift it offered. LED type running lights were now fitted at the front, and redesigned rear light clusters (also LED) were used on Boxster and Cayman to differentiate them externally from the previous models.

Boxster 987
- 2.9-litre (2,893cc) 255bhp (187kW)
- 5-speed manual /7-speed PDK dual clutch transmission
- 17-inch wheels

Boxster S 987
- 3.4-litre (3,387cc) 310bhp (227kW)
- 6-speed manual /7-speed PDK dual clutch transmission
- 18-inch wheels
- Options were as for the 2005 Model Year.

Cayman
- 2.9-litre (2,893cc) 265bhp (195kW)
- 5-speed manual /7-speed PDK dual clutch transmission
- 17-inch wheels

Cayman S
- 3.4-litre (3,387cc) 320bhp (235kW)
- 6-speed manual /7-speed PDK dual clutch transmission
- 18-inch wheels
- Options were similar to the 2007 Model Year, with the notable addition of a limited slip differential now being available.

SPECIAL MODELS

There have been special editions made available of both the Boxster and Cayman at various times. The following were available in most markets.

Boxster S 550 Spyder

The 550 was a limited edition model launched at the end of the 986 model life. This was not quite a "run out" model, as often happens at the end of a model run, since the standard model was always available. The 550 could be specified individually by the customer and was limited to a finite production run of 1953 cars.

The number 1953 was selected as it was the 50th anniversary of the 550 race car, which was produced between 1953 and 1956. As has already been noted, this was the spiritual inspiration for the Boxster concept.

The limited edition was available in only one colour – GT Silver Metallic (which had previously only been offered on the Carrera GT supercar) with a unique cocoa brown full leather interior as standard, with grey natural leather as

Just 1953 examples of the Boxster S 550 Spyder were made

16   Ultimate Owners' Guide

a no-cost option. The power output was increased slightly to 260bhp (191kW) over the standard model, and a host of options were fitted as standard. These included 2-tone grey and silver 18-inch Carrera 5-spoke wheels (with unpainted wheels as no-cost option), 5mm wheel spacers, Sport exhaust with special chrome tip, BOSE sound system, 030 sport suspension (10mm lower), short-shift gearlever and a plate with the limited edition number on the centre console. In the USA the rear lights were all red, whereas the standard 'clear' lights were used on the ROW (rest of the world) cars.

RS60 Spyder

In a similar vein to the Boxster S 550 Spyder, Porsche announced the RS60 Spyder Boxster in November 2007, built to celebrate Porsche's 1960 win in the 12 hours of Sebring race. This edition was limited to 1960 units worldwide with almost half being allocated to the US market. As with the 550 Boxster S, the only paintwork option was GT Silver metallic, with Carrera red leather the standard interior and roof colour (with a dark grey leather interior and black roof available as a no cost option). 19-inch SportDesign wheels (with 5mm spacers) were fitted, along with Porsche's Active Suspension Management (PASM) system. The front used the more pronounced lower lip spoilers of the SportDesign Tecquipment package. A modest increase in engine power to 303bhp (222kW) made it the most powerful Boxster available at the time. A final interior touch was the removal of the cowl over the instrument housing, intending to indicate a more sporting feel to the driving environment. A plaque indicating the number of the particular car from the limited edition was placed on the glovebox lid, and special "RS60 Spyder"

The RS60 limited edition came with 19-inch alloys and PASM

PORSCHE BOXSTER & CAYMAN

Cayman S Porsche Design Edition 1 is themed in black

door entry guards greeted the occupant as they entered the car.

Cayman S Porsche Design Edition 1

Based on the Cayman S of 2008 Model Year, the Design Edition was built commemorating 35th anniversary of Porsche Design, the independent design house that was run by Dr F. A. Porsche in Austria and absorbed back in to the Porsche Group in 2003. There were 777 Design Edition 1 models built, all in black with a black leather interior. Alcantara 'faux suede' covered the steering wheel, gear lever, handbrake grip and roof lining. It featured PASM and 19-inch Turbo wheels. Extra Porsche Design items included were an elegant briefcase containing a 'Flat Six' chronograph watch, a pocket knife, a pair of sunglasses, a pen and a key ring – all in black, even the knife blade.

Boxster Porsche Design Edition 2

Based on the 987 Boxster S, the 2008 Boxster Design Edition 2 was limited to a run of 500. Unusually it was not available in the UK, the model's third largest market. It was painted in Carrara White with light grey 'Porsche Design' stripes over the front and rear lids and doors. There was a black, full leather interior with Carrara White instruments and centre console,

The Boxster Porsche Design Edition 2 in Carrara White/light grey

PORSCHE BOXSTER & CAYMAN

stainless steel door entry guards and a limited edition plaque for the glovebox lid. The steering wheel, gear lever and handbrake were trimmed in Alcantara. The engine had a small power boost over the standard S of the time, with the same 303bhp (222kW) as the RS60. The Design Edition 2 had 19-inch wheels with a twin-outlet sport exhaust.

Each car came with a Porsche Design chronograph watch, the face in Carrara white to match the car.

Cayman S Sport

Announced at the same time as the Boxster S Design Edition 2 (2008), the Cayman S Sport used the same engine and exhaust combination, for the same power and performance. It was available in Orange or Green (as available on the 997 GT3RS of the time) with Cayman S striping along the doors. The wheels were painted black, for a more sporting look, as were the mirrors and air intakes, and the car was equipped with PASM and had 5mm spacers. The interior had the same Alcantara trimmed items against a black leather base. A limited edition plaque was on the glovebox. As with the Boxster RS60 the cowl over the instrument binnacle was deleted. If the colours were not to the taste of the customer, there was the option of Carrara White, Speed Yellow, Guards Red, Black or Arctic Silver. The run was limited to 700.

Boxster and Boxster S Sport Editions

The 987 model had an optional 'Sport Edition' variant available. Based on either model, the Sport Edition featured modified front and rear bumpers that had more pronounced front spoiler lips on the front, and a diffuser design at the rear. The Cayman extending rear wing replaced the standard pop-up spoiler on the rear. All-red tail lights also distinguish it from the standard car. Other features were PASM as standard, a sport steering wheel, and the roll-over hoops painted in body colour. There was no change from the standard models engine outputs.

The Cayman S Sport came in orange or green, but could be specified in less striking colours

KNOWING YOUR CAR

Modern Porsches have a huge number of switches and buttons, and it is possible to fill an entire owners' manual with the full descriptions of what every one does, and where they are. In addition the various versions of the Boxster and Cayman have varied the positions of some controls, some significantly, Porsche relocate items such as the air conditioning depending on options specified, and if you have a pre-owned car it is possible the previous owner has added their own buttons to operate garage door openers, radar detectors, retrofit on-board computer and so on, or even moved some buttons to their own preference! So this chapter will try to orientate the owner with regard to the standard positions of controls and point out some of the differences between the highlighted models.

The Dashboard

Going across the dash (note, right hand drive version shown), from left to right
■ Passenger compartment air vent, with interior temperature sensor below it
■ Loudspeaker on top of dash
■ Airbag, and below it on 2003 Model Year onward cars, a glovebox

The Boxster has a complex arrangement of switches and buttons

22   Ultimate Owners' Guide

Centre air vents, and below them various switchgear, in-car-entertainment and climate controls

■ Hazard flasher switch. Note this is located on central side of the main instrument panel for 986 models and between the centre air vents on the 987.

■ Steering wheel, with main instruments behind

■ Loudspeaker on top of dash

■ Just behind the steering wheel is the ignition key switch

■ Passenger air vent and below it the rotary control for the headlights

The instrument panel

The Boxster has a 3-dial instrument panel, consisting of an analogue speedometer gauge on the left, rev counter in the centre and a combined temperature and fuel gauge on the right.

In the left hand speedometer dial there is also another digital readout. On the early 986 this was a digital odometer (total distance reading) and trip recorder. For 2000-on 986 cars it became the digital speedometer. When the 987 was

A 986 Boxster's dash (above) and below, the later 987 version

Ultimate Owners' Guide 23

PORSCHE BOXSTER & CAYMAN

launched the odometer and trip meter relocated back to the left gauge again!

The centre gauge houses the analogue tachometer (rev counter), the digital display below it can have either the digital speedometer (early 986 and 987/Cayman) or on 2000-on 986 models the odometer and trip, and (if fitted), the on-board-computer readout.

The 987 has the on-board computer located below the speed reading. It also displays the readout from the oil-level sensor when the ignition is first turned on (wait for the countdown to finish for an accurate reading of oil level).

The right hand gauge has the coolant temperature and fuel level (with low fuel warning light), plus a digital clock. If the car is a Tiptronic it also has the gear indicator for the automatic gearbox. 987 models also have the outside air temperature reading in the digital display on the right hand gauge.

Above the instruments are two adjustment buttons (these are relocated to below the instruments on the 987 and Cayman). The left hand one is the trip meter button (push to reset). This doubles as a dimmer control for the instrument illumination.

Instrument illumination is automatically adjusted to take account of different levels via a sensor in the tachometer; however the level you are comfortable with is adjusted by the use of the dimmer control. The right hand button adjusts the time on the digital clock. Press for a second or so until the hour flashes and turn left or right to adjust. Press again and repeat for the minutes. Press a third time to exit adjustment.

On the 986 this control also allows the owner to switch between the display of miles and kilometers on the digital speedometer, odometer (milometer) and trip meter (where fitted). On the 987 this adjustment is managed through the on-board computer. This is essential when (for instance) driving on European roads in a UK car. To do this, turn the adjustment knob to the left for 5 seconds until the display changes. To revert back turn the adjustment to the left again.

Below the instruments on 986 models is a row of warning lights. This row is deleted on the 987 models, with some of the warning lights incorporated in the face of the large central tachometer dial and the airbag and seatbelt warning lights located either side of the central gauge's base. The remainder of the warnings for the 987 models, if triggered, are displayed using the on-board computer display.

On the 986 models, the warning lights are below the gauges

PORSCHE BOXSTER & CAYMAN

On the 987, some of the warning lights are incorporated into the gauge faces

Ultimate Owners' Guide 25

PORSCHE BOXSTER & CAYMAN

Warning Light	Warning shown on 987	Warning shown on 987 OBC
Washer fluid level light		
Emission Control warning light		
Porsche Stability Management (PSM) information light		
Porsche Stability Management (PSM) warning light		
ABS warning light		

Warning Light	Warning shown on 987	Warning shown on 987 OBC
Brake-fluid warning light	Combined in to a single warning graphic. In the USA the graphic is replaced with the word "BRAKE"	
Handbrake warning light		
Brake-pad wear warning light		
Engine oil pressure warning light		
Battery charge warning light		

Centre Console

In all models, the centre console houses the heating and ventilation controls (be it just a heater, air conditioning or climate control (dependant on the options specified) and the in-car entertainment (ICE - whether cassette/radio, CD/radio, or Porsche Communications Management (PCM) GPS satellite navigation).

The centre console arrangement in the Boxster and Cayman can have many different layouts depending which of the air conditioning, climate control, Digital Sound Plus, satellite navigation

Ultimate Owners' Guide

PORSCHE BOXSTER & CAYMAN

Warning Light	Warning shown on 987	Warning shown on 987 OBC
Seat belt warning light	🔴	⬛
Airbag warning light	🔴	⬛
Retractable spoiler warning light		⬛
Luggage compartment lids open warning light		⬛
Convertible top indicator lights		⬛

Warning Light	Warning shown on 987	Warning shown on 987 OBC
General warning light (other faults)	!	See 'info' menu on OBC
Tyre Pressure monitoring System (TPS)	⚠	See 'info' menu on OBC

NOTE:
When the ignition is turned on the lamps light up for a bulb check. The on-board computer also displays many other warnings depending on the triggering event. These include PASM, service indicators and detailed TPC information. If the Sport Chrono option is fitted, other display events are shown.

options are fitted. For example on 986 models the fitment of the GPS satellite navigation (PCM) module means that the climate control panel is relocated to the lower half of the console, from its original position at the very top.

The lower half of the console on 986 models could be deleted altogether. This option was particularly useful for taller drivers, giving a little extra room for the knees. The 987 does not have the option to delete the lower console, however the pedals are set a little further away giving more legroom. This comes at some expense to the shorter driver though

Ultimate Owners' Guide **27**

PORSCHE BOXSTER & CAYMAN

– who has to sit that little bit further forward. In this case, the steering wheel/gearstick/handbrake relationships are now not optimal for the shorter driver. I'm not so tall (unfortunately!) and personally I find the 987 uncomfortable compared to the 986 because of this.

Around the main modules in the upper centre console of the 986 are some switches. These can consist of a selection of the following, dependant on the options specified:
- Porsche Stability Management (PSM) control
- Footwell lights
- Central locking
- Door mirror (and rear window with hardtop) heating
- Convertible top operation

There may be one or more blanks if you do not have some of the options listed or alternatively, you may find that a previous owner has added a switch or two for other non-standard functions.

Most of these switches are relocated to

The 986 centre dash, with central locking, heated rear window and convertible top buttons arranged on the left side of the climate control panel

PORSCHE BOXSTER & CAYMAN

Centre dash arrangement of the 987 with climate controls at centre

the bottom of the lower centre console in the 987, except the heated rear window/ door mirrors switch, which is among the climate control unit switch array.

Below the switches on the upper centre console of the 986, there is an accessory power socket (with a cigar lighter normally fitted). This may be a blanking plate if the 'No-smoker' option was selected by the original owner. Opposite this, on post 2000 MY cars, is a rheostat (variable output switch) that allows the interval of the intermittent wipers to be adjusted.

The lower switches on the 987 centre console consist of:
- Rear spoiler,
- Porsche Active Suspension Management (PASM),
- Sport Mode,
- Porsche Stability Management (PSM),
- Sports exhaust system

Again it is likely that some of these switches will not be present, as they depend on the actual options fitted.

If you are wondering where the convertible roof operation switch went on the 987 it is next to the handbrake (parking brake).

Light Switch
The Boxster's lighting is controlled by a rotary switch and the graphics around the rim show the lights selected (sidelights, headlights, etc.). To operate the front and rear fog lights you pull the switch out one click (fronts) and two clicks (adds rear fog lights).

The 987 also has the option of a 'Home' function, allowing the front foglights and rear tail lights to stay on for 30 seconds after you exit and lock the car (giving you time to find your doorkeys etc). This option is not available in all territories.

Steering wheel adjustment
The 986 only has adjustment for reach (forwards and backwards). This oversight was finally rectified with the introduction of the 987 when vertical adjustment was added. To adjust the wheel there is a locking lever beneath the wheel.

Rear console
The rear console has a locking storage box. In pre-2003 models this is the only locking storage in the interior. Incidentally the most common cause of the alarm 'beeping' when you lock the car is that the lid of the storage box is not latched – it is easy to hit the lock with your elbow whilst driving, thereby accidentally triggering the latch. (See the electrics

Ultimate Owners' Guide

PORSCHE BOXSTER & CAYMAN

986 centre console with window and heated seat controls around the ashtray

and Caymans also had a power socket at the passenger side of the centre console (in the footwell). However this was soon deleted as a standard fitment and is now only available if the Bose sound system is specified when ordering.

Luggage net/Storage Box/ Bose base port

Above the engine cover, below the roll-hoops there is either a luggage net, luggage bag, or storage box (dependant on the specification ordered). If the Bose sound system has been specified then the storage box is replaced by a Bose subwoofer port.

Other controls

Porsche have a continuous programme of development and this seems to mean that an analogous programme of adding controls goes along with it. This book just does not have space to cover all the options and functions of modules such as the In Car Entertainment (in its many different variants), climate control,

chapter for more alarm information).

Forward of the rear console is the ashtray. 986 models have the electric window switches forward of the ashtray, and (optionally) the switches for the heated seats behind. On the 987 the window switches are on the doors, and the heated seat switches at either end of the climate control switches in the lower centre console.

The 987 has a power socket/cigar lighter in the ashtray. Very early 987s satellite navigation, multi-function steering wheel, seat memory controls and so on. Thankfully, these are all mostly logical in operation, and in any case are not central to the control and operation of the car. Have fun exploring your car!

Fuses and relays

We stay inside the passenger compartment in order to locate the fuses and relays. The fuses are under a plastic panel in the carpet between the driver's feet and the door. Simply pull the panel out using the hole in the front. There is a fold-out fuse cross-reference tucked inside the pull-off panel. There are also instructions on how to open the front luggage compartment if you have a dead battery.

The relays are tucked away up above the fuse panel.

These are not exactly easy to see and deal with. The easiest (!) way to see what you are dealing with here is to lay upside down with your head in the footwell.

The fuse panel is tucked away in the right side footwell, note fuse chart in cover

PORSCHE BOXSTER & CAYMAN

There are more relays in the rear boot – accessed behind the carpet on the opposite side of the boot to the Oil/Water service area.

See the Electrics Chapter for further Information.

Front luggage compartment

The front and rear compartments can of course be opened with the appropriate buttons on the key, and you will likely have already found those, but there are also switches located on the door sill next to the driver's seat. On the early cars these are lever operated but for the 2001 model year these were changed to touch switches. Either way they will only operate if the car has sufficient battery power. If the battery is flat, it is important to know how to get into the front compartment (especially). This emergency opening situation is covered in the Body chapter.

As well as giving access to the battery, opening the front compartment gives access to the load area, the emergency wheel (available with the 986 only),

Front compartment gives access to battery and emergency wheel (986 only)

toolkit, CD Changer (if fitted) and the brake fluid reservoir.

Screenwash

Next to the battery is the cap for the screenwash reservoir. For cars fitted with Litronic (Xenon) headlights this doubles as the headlight cleaner reservoir and is of a larger capacity than the screenwash-only version.

Fuel filler

The fuel filler is on the right hand front wing or fender. It is locked when you lock the car, but free to open and allow access to the filler cap otherwise. If you find it remains locked when the car itself is unlocked, there is an emergency cable operated by a pull ring located in the door jamb behind the flap (this cable is visible only with the door open).

PORSCHE BOXSTER & CAYMAN

The fuel filler is located in the right front wing/fender. Note cap hook!

A nice touch that Porsche designed in is a little hook on the inside of the filler flap, this allows you to hang the petrol cap away from the bodywork using the rubber strap attached to the cap. Early cars did not have this strap, but it is available from Porsche for a small cost.

The rear luggage compartment

Inside the rear luggage compartment you will find the remaining 'self service' items, the oil and water fillers and on 986 models, the oil dipstick (987 and Cayman models rely solely on the digital oil level display in the instrument dials).

On the 986 and 987 these service items are located in plain sight on the right top side of the compartment. On Cayman and later 987 models they are hidden under a flap in the same area.

On the opposite side of the rear luggage area, behind the carpet, is the second relay panel. This contains the relays for the components located to the rear of the car such as rear spoiler extension, DME relay, starter motor, etc.

Ultimate Owners' Guide **33**

PORSCHE BOXSTER & CAYMAN

Using a floor jack

Every now and again you may want to get a good look under your car, or jack it up to remove the wheels at home rather than in an emergency at the side of the road.

For these situations a hydraulic floor jack is invaluable. The supplied jack is for emergencies only – I would not want to entrust it to multiple lifts and lowers of a heavy car.

If you are buying a hydraulic jack, get one with a low insertion height (the minimum height of the lifting pad from the ground) – the Boxster is surprisingly low and it is better to buy a jack that fits under without problem, rather than having to mess around driving on to planks of wood to get enough clearance for the jack to fit.

I have glued a chunk of old rubber floor mat to the top of my jack to avoid damaging the paint on the jack points – others use an ice-hockey puck in place of this to achieve the same effect.

Self service items (oil yellow, coolant blue) in the 986 rear compartment

34   Ultimate Owners' Guide

On the Cayman, the service fillers are under a flap. Note the lack of an engine oil dipstick – in common with all the 987 models

Ultimate Owners' Guide

EMERGENCIES

Things to get you out of trouble

Firstly, what might you need to know if you find yourself stranded? Well, it is recommend you obtain some sort of breakdown cover regardless of how adept you feel in tackling problems yourself, there are many things that are just not easy to fix, and indeed some that only an Official Porsche Centre, or Porsche specialist with the correct diagnostic equipment can fully rectify. Nonetheless you can help yourself with a little orientation exercise in getting to know your car:

There's no tool kit?

Well, not visible anyway. For the 986, the tool kit and jack can be found inside the back of the emergency space-saver wheel. The spare wheel is only supplied with the 986 Boxster (pre-2004 model year) - the 987 that succeeded it does not come with one as the 19" wheel/tyres fitted at the rear are so wide that a punctured tyre just will not fit in the front luggage area. 987s come with a can of tyre sealant instead. The spare wheel in 986s is held to the rear of the luggage compartment with a large butterfly nut that is unscrewed by hand. To get to the butterfly nut you need to put your hand inside the middle of the cover that is fitted over the spare wheel and simply unscrew the nut. You can now pull the spare wheel off the protruding bolt, and locate the jack and toolkit that are hidden away inside the bowl of the wheel, inside a formed polystyrene moulding.

The polystyrene moulding holds:
- An Emergency jack for lifting the vehicle for tyre changing
- Speed-brace for the jack

The 986 emergency wheel houses the warning triangle and other tools

36 Ultimate Owners' Guide

The polystyrene moulding holds the jack and speed brace, plus (right) the tool roll, gloves, etc.

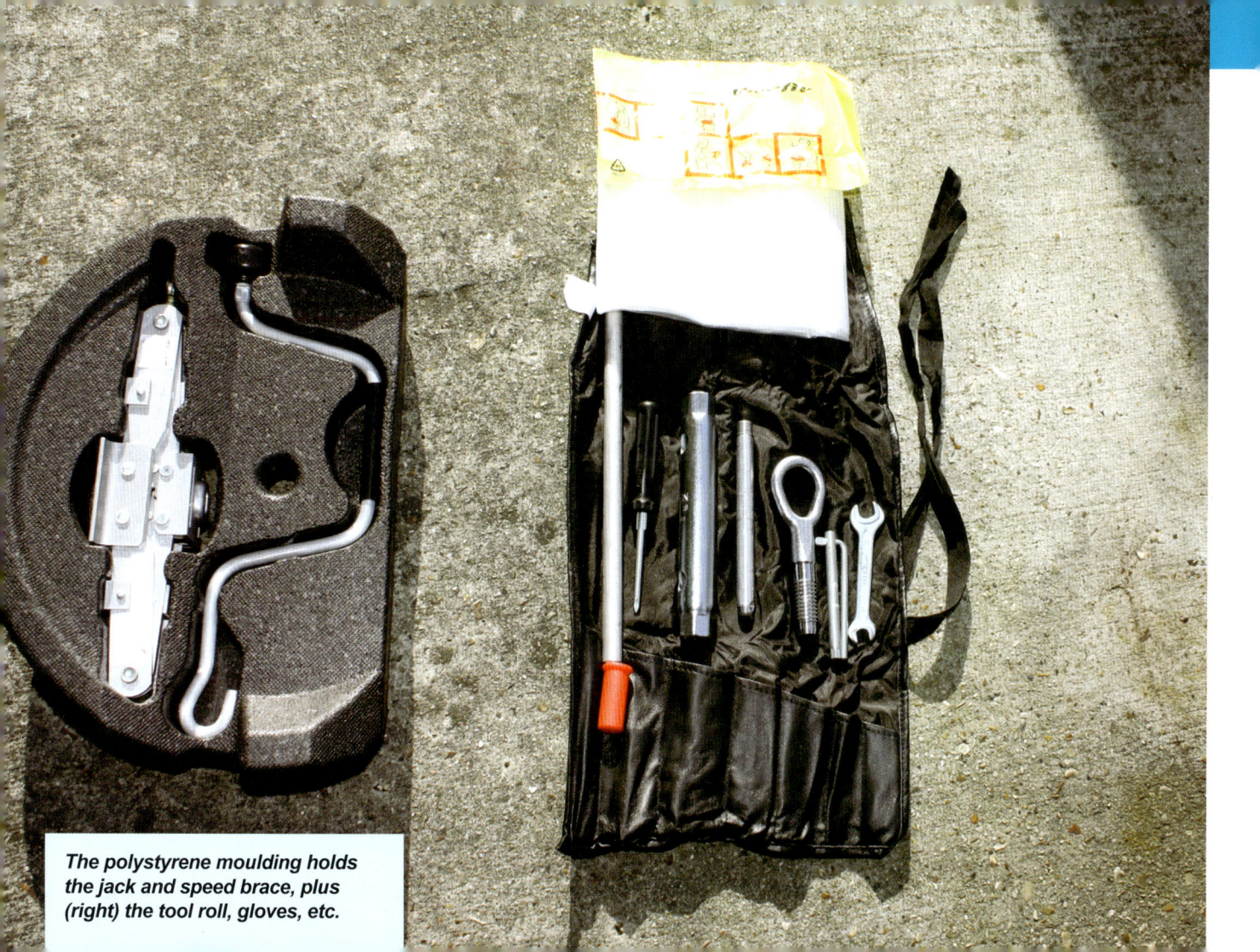

PORSCHE BOXSTER & CAYMAN

The Toolroll contains
- Lever for convertible top emergency operation – This doubles as a lever for the wheel-bolt spanner/wrench
- Double-ended screwdriver
- Wheel bolt spanner/wrench
- Guide bar for wheel changing
- Towing Eye
- Headlight socket wrench
- Small spanner
- Disposable plastic gloves

In the 987/Cayman the toolkit is at the bottom-rear of the front boot, under a plastic cover. (Under the panel the emergency triangle is mounted on in the photograph).

This should contain:
- The adapter for security wheel bolts
- A tyre filling compressor
- Towing hook
- Tool roll

- Lever for convertible top emergency operation (under the tool roll)
- A can of tyre sealant

The toolroll contains
- Lever for convertible top emergency operation
- Double-ended screwdriver
- Guide bar for wheel changing (x2 if the car is fitted with PCCB brakes)
- Towing eye

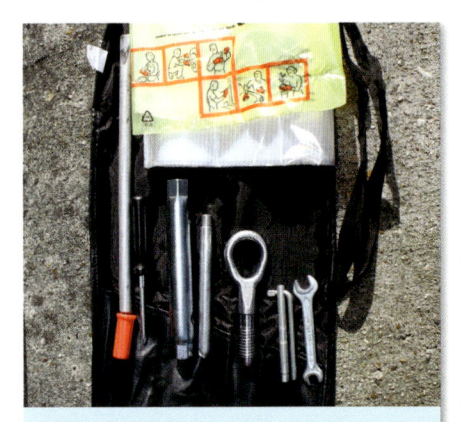

The basic toolkit includes a wheelbolt wrench and towing eye

The more basic tool inventory for the 987, with inflation compressor (left)

38 Ultimate Owners' Guide

PORSCHE BOXSTER & CAYMAN

- Headlight socket wrench
- Small spanner
- Disposable plastic gloves

"I've got a flat battery - How do I get to it?"

Inside the front luggage compartment you will find the battery. This is hidden away under a plastic cover located in the centre of the top of the luggage area (between the luggage area and the base of the windscreen). However if the battery is flat the levers or switches that operate the release do not work – The levers are cable operated but a solenoid locks them closed, and the switches will only operate if the car has sufficient battery power, so you need another way to get the front and rear compartments open in the event of a flat battery

How do I get in then…?

On early cars there is no visible way to get the front boot open with a flat battery. Bit of an oversight there Porsche… But wait, there is a technical bulletin that covers how to do it - not that helpful to the owner who doesn't normally have access to such things.

First unlock the car using the key and leave the key in the door lock.

Take the fuse box cover off (see the next section). Take a look inside and look for a red covered post (the red cover slides out) with a graphic of the front

Connect the positive jumper cable to the red pull-out post

Ultimate Owners' Guide   39

boot open on it. If you have this then things are a little easier – if not then you have one of the early cars, no matter the procedure is very similar.

If you have the red post then inside the cover of the fuse cover there should also be a fold-out sheet with instructions on how to open the boot. If the piece of paper is missing then this is what you do:

■ Get a spare battery and a set of jump leads, connect the positive of the donor battery to the pull-out post.

■ Connect the negative lead to the latch striker in the door opening. Be prepared for the alarm to go off (if it hasn't already gone off when you unlocked the car and opened the door).

■ Switch the alarm off by locking and unlocking the door lock.

■ Unlock the luggage compartment using the lever or switch.

■ Disconnect the negative cable first, then the positive.

■ Push the pull-out terminal back in to the Fuse Box and replace the cover.

Connect the negative jumper cable to the door striker latch

If you do not have the red post then the Porsche Technical Bulletin advises:
- Open the door.
- Using an external battery, connect the negative lead to the door stop.
- Connect the positive lead to both sides of fuse "C3".
- With the door open, move the door latch with a screwdriver into the closed position.
- Using the key, lock and unlock the door.
- The front and rear hood releases can now be operated.

> **WARNING:**
> ⚠ In no case should any attempt be made to start the engine using any of the methods listed here – the current through the terminals is insufficient and you risk expensive damage.

Another way that can be tried is using an accessory socket type trickle charger (this will need to be powered on for at least an hour before attempting to unlock the boot).

There is also an emergency cable release hidden away under the right hand (when sitting in the drivers seat) front wheel arch liner on 986s and the left hand liner on 987s. However it is not really designed to be used by the owner – being almost impossible to locate, and pull – in reality a wheel would need to be removed to even see the little cut-out that is provided for access to the cable, and how are you going to do that if the puzzle lock (wheelbolt lock socket) is hidden away in the front luggage area…(hint – keep it in the passenger area – mine is in the "ashtray"!). My thought on this is that the cable is actually provided in case one of the solenoids or electrical actuators that opens the luggage compartment fails.

Some owners have re-routed the cable to a more accessible location – behind the towing eye panel, but this means removing the front bumper cover to do this - which is no good if you are stuck right now.

Note that a similar emergency cable is also fitted to the rear compartment.

Jacking the car – using the emergency wheel

Firstly, as indicated earlier, only the 986 comes with a jack and emergency (spare) wheel. The 987 just has a can of tyre sealant to use if you get a puncture.

If you do get a puncture and are going to be using the emergency wheel then first try and get the car to level, firm ground.

The supplied jack must only be used in the 4 locations specified by Porsche (2 each side).

It is not designed to support anywhere else and is only for emergencies. It isn't designed to support the car for any longer than the time it takes to change a wheel.

Ensure that you have firmly applied the handbrake, put the car in gear, and if possible wedge something each side of the wheels on the side that you are not working on to prevent the car rolling when you jack it up.

Slacken the wheel bolts before lifting the car, then jack up. Remove one of the nuts completely and insert the guide bar from the tool kit. The guide bar is used to help locate the wheel on to the hub. This helps to prevent knocking the wheel against the brake disc and in so doing scratching or damaging the wheel.

Important – PCCB Brakes! If you have PCCB brakes then it is even more important to use the guide bar as knocking the wheel against the disc could actually break the disc. In fact Porsche supply 2 guide bars to cars fitted with PCCB and both should be used on each wheel.

Remove remaining nuts and wheel.

Note: If you have spacers fitted these must also be used with the space saver wheel, so do not remove these.

Before replacing the wheel bolts the thread and spherical cap surface should be cleaned, and a thin coat of Optimoly TA (an aluminium paste grease) applied on the thread, and between the bolt head and the spherical cap. Note that the rounded area that tightens against the wheel must not be greased.

Put the replacement wheel on, hand tightening the bolts, Remove the guide bar and replace the bolt. Lower the car and when the weight of the car is back on it, finish tightening the wheel bolts in a diagonal (opposite) pattern.

After changing a wheel, check the tightening torque – it should be 130 Nm/96 ftlb. Do not exceed this.

Ensure the lug on the jack top is located in the mating hole

PORSCHE BOXSTER & CAYMAN

The guide bar is an essential aid to prevent damage to the wheel and brake

Ultimate Owners' Guide 43

BODYSHELL CARE

The Boxster is a roadster configuration mid-engined sports car with 2 seats and an electrically powered folding fabric roof. The 2 luggage areas provide the ability to carry enough luggage for 2 people for a 2-week touring holiday, with the bonus amusement factor of seeing the unbelieving look on people's faces when they see you put a couple of suitcases in the front and then another one in the back… (More than once I've been asked where the engine is – in reply I sometimes ask if they have seen The Flintstones…?).

The 986 and 987 variants look very similar in what seems to be a continuing Porsche policy to evolve slowly the look of the cars they make. It means that many unfamiliar with the model do not realise there are actually differences. The 987 has flatter, less sculpted doors, flattened edges to the wheelarches, redesigned front and rear lights and more dramatic looking side intakes. In fact there is not a panel on the body that hasn't been changed between the 986 and 987. Nevertheless, Porsche have successfully managed to keep the same overall look.

The Cayman inherits all the design elements from the 987, adding a fixed roof and an opening tailgate for rear luggage access. Personally, I feel the design changes that were made to the 987 suit the Cayman better, with the Boxster suffering some styling elements implemented for the Cayman that are not so well suited to the open-topped version. But perhaps that is an argument that should be reserved for those times when owners are gathered for a friendly debate in a pub!

Construction and safety

The Boxster series uses an all-steel unitary construction bodyshell. Under the taut lines of the body are safety features such as front and rear deformation zones that progressively absorb impacts and rigid side structures to help prevent side intrusion. The windscreen frame and roll-over bars (on the Boxster) provide protection in the case of an inversion. Porsche refer to the windscreen frame and many elements of the underbody as being in 'high-strength steel', or 'super high-strength steel'. The roll-over hoops are formed in a high strength stainless steel. The bumpers at front and rear are in reality bumper covers made from Polypropylene-ethylene-propylene-diene-monomer (thankfully this is usually shortened to PPEPDM, and for the non-chemists amongst us, more often referred to as just plain 'PU'). The actual bumpers themselves are hidden underneath these covers and consist of 5mm thick

Strong aluminium bumpers are hidden under the deformable plastic covers

44　Ultimate Owners' Guide

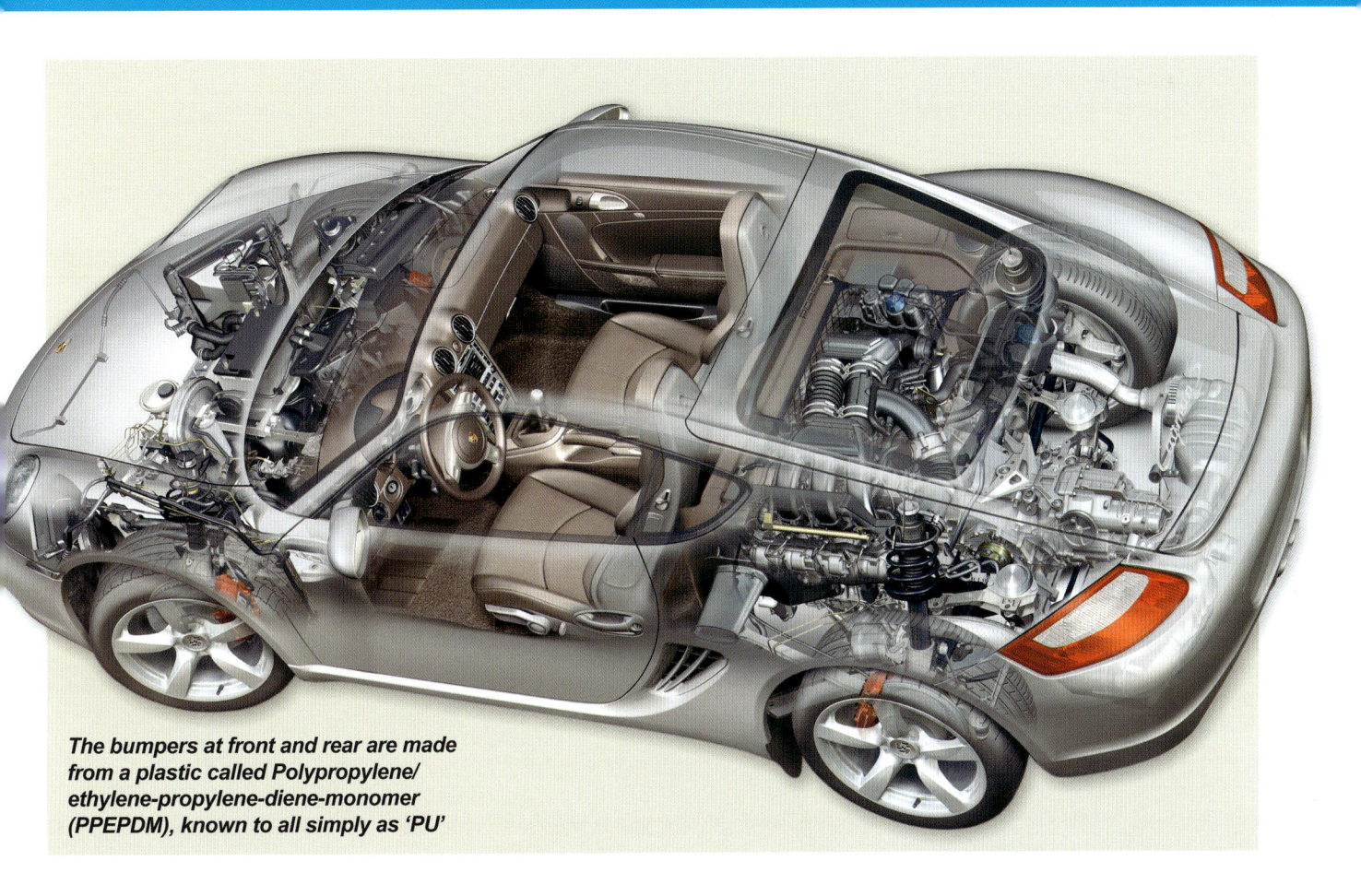

The bumpers at front and rear are made from a plastic called Polypropylene/ethylene-propylene-diene-monomer (PPEPDM), known to all simply as 'PU'

Ultimate Owners' Guide   45

PORSCHE BOXSTER & CAYMAN

extruded aluminium beams attached to the bodyshell by telescoping impact absorbers.

The 987 and Cayman replaced the steel front and rear luggage compartment covers with aluminium versions to assist with weight saving.

Convertible roof operation

The Boxster's convertible roof is operated by first engaging the handbrake (pre-2003MY 986 only) and then unlatching the release lever at the front of the roof. To do this press in the centre of the lever and it will pop out into position. Pull the lever to the rear as far as it will go. The windows will also lower a small amount to allow the roof to clear them during lowering.

Now leave the release lever at the rearmost 'open' position and use the rocker switch to open the roof – the rocker switch is in the upper centre console on the 986 and next to the handbrake in the 987. Keep the rocker switch held in through the entire operation on the 986, and up to 6mph (10km/h) on the 987. If above 6mph – and below 30 mph

The Boxster's roof is opened first by unlatching the release lever (at right, below)

46 Ultimate Owners' Guide

(48km/h) – then a single touch on the switch will set the operation going. When the roof is fully lowered the light in the instrument panel will extinguish and the operation is complete.

With Boxsters that have a plastic rear window, the convertible roof should not be opened in cold weather as the plastic can split. See the section below for a method of opening the roof with least stress to the plastic window.

Sadly, Cayman owners have to resort to other ways to open the roof of their cars – an angle grinder being a useful accessory for a single-time-only opening.

To close the roof on a 986 manufactured before the 2003MY, stop the car and engage the handbrake. Operate the roof rocker switch – holding it in until the roof indicator light goes out on the early 986s and on 987s if below 6 mph. To close the roof on a 987 travelling above 6 mph, you only have to briefly touch the rocker switch.

When the roof has closed completely, move the release lever to the front again, ensuring that the hook at the front engages in the windscreen rail. The windows will close fully.

Note: Do not attempt to open or close the roof above 30 mph in the 987. It will not operate. Driving with the roof partially open above 30 mph will damage it – and may even cause loss of control of the car.

Always make sure that there is nothing to get in the way of the roof mechanism or power windows when operating the convertible top. Hint: Do not lean in through the window to latch the top – ouch!

Front bumper removal/ accessing the radiators

Every now and again it becomes necessary to give the radiators and air conditioning heat-exchangers

The air conditioning heat exchangers are mounted ahead of the coolant radiators, ahead of each front wheel

(condensers) a good clean. As mentioned elsewhere you can get at them from out side of the car with a vacuum cleaner adapted with a crevice tool fashioned from a cardboard tube, but to give them a really good clean you need to get the front bumper off. This is not as bad a job as you might fear, and can be completed at home in 2-3 hours.

The procedure described here is for a 2001 Boxster S. There are slight differences between model years but the basic principles should be similar. The same process also works on the 996 series.

Tools and Parts
You will need the following:
- 10mm socket
- 19mm socket
- T25 and T30 Torx bits
- Flat blade screwdriver
- Philips Screwdriver bit
- Floor Jack
- Jack Stands
- Torque Wrench
- Wheel Bolt puzzle lock key (locking wheelnut socket)
- Vacuum cleaner – wet and dry would be best

→ SAFETY FIRST!

To service the car it will be necessary to raise one side of the car off the ground and for this you will need a trolley (garage service) jack rated at 1.5 tonnes (3,300lb) or more that will start at a height of about 80mm (3 inches) and lift to around 400mm (16 inches). Finally, you will need a pair of good axle stands each having four feet.

THIS MAY BE STATING THE OBVIOUS – BUT NEVERTHELESS:
- Make sure the car is on level, solid ground out of the way of traffic and passers-by
- Turn the front wheels in the direction you need before you lift
- Place blocks under the opposite side wheels so the car can't roll – don't rely on the handbrake
- Once the stands are located properly, let the jack down slightly so that the stands cannot move – then check them again
- If you feel safer leaving the hydraulic jack in place, don't leave the jack handle horizontal for someone to hit or trip over – or remove it if it won't park vertically
- If you are venturing below, wear eye protection – grit and rust flakes are no fun
- Don't run the engine while under the car

You won't need any new parts but it might be useful to obtain some new plastic "expansion rivets" before you start – there are several each side and they can be broken on removal. You will want to have some spare just in case. The part number for these is 999 507 497 40.

You will also want to have a willing assistant handy when you remove and refit the bumper cover itself – it can be awkward to handle and is easy to scratch.

Remove the wheel arch liners
The first thing is to remove the wheel arch liners – I have to say that it is possible to remove the bumper without doing this but access is far more difficult. It is easier to remove the liners, or at least just the front of them.

First jack the front of the car up on one side and remove the wheel. For safety remember to support the car with a jack stand in a suitable place before working under the car.

The wheelarch liner has several expansion rivets and 3 plastic nuts visible in the wheel arch – remove these. The plastic nuts unscrew easily with the 10mm socket, however the expansion rivets can be, shall we say "variable", in the ease of removal… You are supposed to pull the top back out of the rivet, and you may

The wheelarch liner is located with plastic rivets and nuts

The expansion rivets can be difficult to remove

Ultimate Owners' Guide **49**

find on some you can do this with just your fingers; others will prove rather more reluctant to move. You may find that the flat blade of a screwdriver levers the top up enough to get them out, I found that I needed to work some needle nose pliers under the partially lifted top and work the pin out. I bet Porsche have a special tool for this (or they just get the apprentice to break his fingernails removing them!).

Under the front of the bumper there is another plastic rivet to remove – this is in a little recess and difficult to get hold of. You can't even see it from directly in front of the car.

Next you need to remove the plastic flap in front of the wheelarch, and the small scoop if fitted (the scoop is on the S only) using a Philips head screwdriver, and a T30 Torx for the fixing at the front of the scoop (this is still present if you don't have the scoop – it is at the front of the hole in front of the plastic flap – and also holds the bumper on – so still needs to be removed anyway).

Note that the 987 has the flaps built in to the wheelarch liner – they are not a separate component.

Finally undo two T30 Torx screws under the very corner of the bumper which were half hidden by the plastic flap.

Now you can remove the wheelarch liner – this can be a struggle as it is a very tight fit – it will come out though with a bit of flexing of the plastic (so possibly best not to do it in very cold temperatures!).

Removing the rivet from behind the front bumper underside isn't easy either!

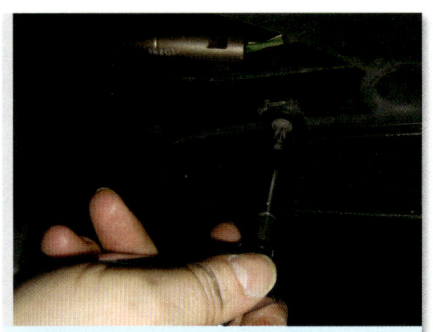

Removing the plastic flap and small scoop in front of the wheelarch

You'll need a T30 Torx driver to undo the fasteners under the bumper at the front of the scoop

PORSCHE BOXSTER & CAYMAN

Remove Sidelights and fixings
Now you have the wheelarch liner out you can remove 3 screws under the sidelight. To do this first remove the sidelight (see the section on bulb replacement for details).

Once you have the sidelight housing off, just twist the bulb-holder and leave the bulb, holder and loom attached to the car. Place the sidelight housing safely aside.

There are 3 screws to remove, one at the front of the sidelight recess, one in the top rear of the recess (vertical) and one behind the bumper into the lower of the sidelight area. – see the pictures for details. Note these screws have some shaped washers that are fitted with them – Porsche refer to them as spacers but they are not that far short of dished washers!

It is actually just the last screw behind the bumper that requires the front of the wheel arch liner to be removed for access. You might find you can access it by removing just the expansion rivets in this area and pulling the liner away for access – but getting your hand in here would be quite painful.

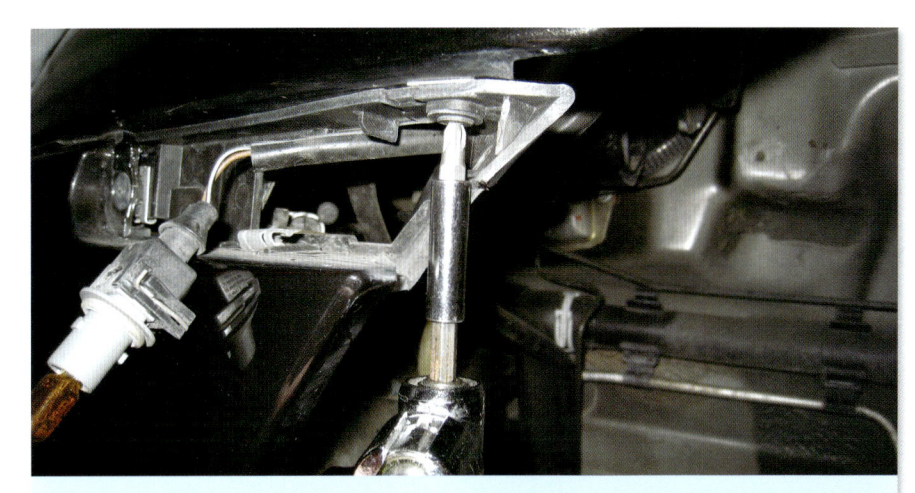

Removing the sidelights and fixings: attached by three screws (above, below)

Note that your model year might not have all 3 of these screws, or they may not be in the same places.

Repeat for the other side
Now you need to do the other side. If you wish and are confident you can jack the other side up with this side supported on the jack stand – however I am wary of the way the jack I have moves the car as

Ultimate Owners' Guide

it raises it – so I put the wheel back on for now and lower the car back on to the wheels.

Remaining bumper fixings
Once you have removed the wheelarch liner on each side, remove 3 more T30 Torx screws under the front centre of the bumper, and that is all the lower fixings taken care of.

Open the front luggage compartment and remove the plastic trim around the catch at the front. There are four plastic fasteners that remove by turning through 90°. Then pull the plastic from under the rubber seal and over the release lever.

Remove 2 screws in the top of the bumper – note how the bumper slots into the adjacent parts for when you refit it.

Unclip the temperature probe from the grill in the front right (looking forward) – this just pushes out.

I find it easier to remove the headlights for visibility, and as it only takes seconds to do I would – but this is not compulsory. See the section on bulb replacement for instructions.

Remove the bumper
Now it is time for your willing assistant (they don't have to be willing but it helps) to join you and you can slide the bumper off. If it won't come off check that there are no more fixings that have not been removed – it is easy to miss one or two, or your model may not have exactly the same layout as the one shown here.

Place something soft on the ground to avoid scratching the bumper on removal. Get hold of the bumper at a corner each and slide the bumper forwards and off. Place it somewhere safe where it will not get scratched. In the photograph it is resting on a mechanic's mat on initial removal, before going somewhere softer to lay on!

Remove the radiator scoops
The radiators and air conditioning heat-exchangers have plastic/rubber scoops directing air to them from the grilles in the front bumper. These are held on with T25 Torx screws. Remove the screws – there are 2 on the outside at the rear of the scoops, 2 inside the front of the scoops

and one at the top just under the headlight (or where the headlight would be if you removed it).

With these removed the scoops will be detachable, but remember that the one on the right has the temperature probe attached. If you need to get the scoop away from the car push the grommet (the rubber plug that the probe's wires go through) out of the scoop – and the probe can fit through the grommet hole.

Remove the scoop. You should now have a lot of debris on the garage floor which has fallen out of the scoop. So, time to get the vacuum cleaner out. Don't use the one that is used for normal household cleaning, or you will likely not be popular with your partner. This book is supposed to save you money, and divorces are not cheap.

Vacuum all around the radiators and heat exchangers (condensers). While you have access, you may want to give them a rinse through with a hose (but not a pressure washer – you might damage the cores).

This is probably all you need to do to

PORSCHE BOXSTER & CAYMAN

Four plastic half-turn fasteners hold the front trim in the front compartment (top left). Remove the top two screws from the bumper (left) and have an assistant help slide the bumper forwards and off the car on to a soft surface

Ultimate Owners' Guide   53

PORSCHE BOXSTER & CAYMAN

There are two T25 Torx screws holding each condenser

The second condenser retaining screw is at the base

remove the debris and clean them up, but you can separate the heat exchangers from the radiators if you feel you need to – there are two Torx fixings to the inboard side of the heat exchangers and you can slide the assembly towards the centre of the car to separate them from the radiators. Just make sure that the rubber tubing that they are attached with is flexing rather than the aluminium tubing.

I've never needed to do this, however if you find lots of debris clogging in the radiators you might wish to do so.

The centre radiator can be vacuumed out in the same way as before. I've never needed to remove the plastic cowling around it to do so.

Reassembly
Reassembly really is the reverse of disassembly, but there are a few hints I have found to help.

When you slide the bumper back in to position make sure it lines up correctly (remember noting how it fitted on the top? – make sure it slides in between the two flat surfaces).

You might find the bumper will not go on – which doesn't make sense… This can result in much frustration and comments from the aforesaid willing assistant, who didn't know why you needed to remove the stupid bumper in the first place.

54 Ultimate Owners' Guide

PORSCHE BOXSTER & CAYMAN

Scoop removed and debris. This condenser is also showing a leak and should be replaced as well

Let me save you that situation – what has probably happened is that the rubber scoops have dropped down slightly – especially if you have had the bumper off for a couple of days. They tend to drop and interfere with the bumper being able to slide in to place, but you can't see this. To cure this issue simply use your fingers through the top slot of the bumper grilles to push the rubber scoops up – the bumper will slide on.

The wheelarch liner can be difficult to replace. Again, it will flex a little to allow it to "pop" in to place. Make sure it fits into position above the return of the wheelarch flange.

Lastly the expansion rivets that were difficult to remove can be just as difficult to replace. The holes they are going into obviously need to line up or you will have difficulty pushing the pin into place, but even then they can be difficult. A tiny drop of spray lubricant will allow you to ease the pin into place much easier.

Make sure you remember to check the headlight assembly is located securely and that all lights and sidelights work correctly.

Finally torque the wheelbolts to 130 Nm (96 lbft).

Problem areas:
Corrosion

Thankfully the Boxster seems to have escaped common problem areas that cause corrosion. The issues that have caused rust to take hold on previous Porsche models are generally absent from the Boxster range. There is just one area that has been a common problem on early cars, and that is fairly small: rusting of the body under the door striker (door catch) on early cars.

The door striker or catch was originally bolted directly to the finished paintwork. The edges of its base can be sharp and cut through the protective paint, damaging the paint and protective treatment and allowing corrosion to form. This can

Ultimate Owners' Guide

PORSCHE BOXSTER & CAYMAN

A bad case of corrosion under a door striker plate

Clearing the drain points (protecting Alarm Module)

There is a glaring omission in the factory owner's handbook that is supplied with the Boxster. There is no mention of the fact that there are several drain points that allow water to safely drain out of the car and which really do need to be kept clear. Why do they need to be kept clear? Well, if they are not, the water has nowhere to go and in certain circumstances will find another route to the lowest point it can find in the car. It will just sit there.

Unfortunately this low point is usually beneath the seats. This is not just a case of the carpets getting damp and a little smelly, but often it results in a much more expensive problem. The main Alarm Control Module is mounted under the left hand seat and if it sits in water for any protracted length of time it will invariably fail or start to act in unpredictable ways – and it's expensive to replace.

The official Porsche method of clearing the drain points is to blow in to each drain point with a compressed-air line. The average owner isn't likely to have a high-pressure airline handy, so another method will need to be employed. The accompanying photographs show the location of the drain-points. Vacuum them first if necessary to remove loose debris. If they are fitted (from around 2000 Porsche decided the drain pipes were superfluous) the pipes themselves can be quite complex, so just pushing a stiff wire down them probably won't work. For example, the centre front drain can have a drain tube with 4 90° bends in it – this will be difficult to negotiate and you don't want to push the tube off its mounting grommet, nor tear the tube itself. Try something flexible but non-damaging to ensure a clear path.

If you have the tubes, ensure that whatever you use to clear the drain tubes will not cause damage – you don't want to risk ripping them and allowing the water to drain into areas they are designed to route water away from. Of course any leaves or other debris should be routinely cleared away from the drain points as well – or they will block them just as easily.

Note there are three drain points in

happen particularly if the plate has been moved to adjust the latch point for any reason.

After several years production (believed to be around MY 2000) a flexible gasket was introduced between the latch and the paintwork, thereby protecting the paint and preventing the damage that could allow corrosion to start.

Ultimate Owners' Guide

total in the front of the car (under the trim panels either side of the battery). In the back there is one each side under the convertible top trim panel.

986 lower flaps and handling

Along with tyres and suspension alignment (see elsewhere) there is something else that can affect the stability and perceived handling of the car – the little flaps that hang down in front of the front wheels. These serve multiple purposes including helping to extract hot air from the radiators. They are the first thing that touches when negotiating a ramp so give an audible warning – as long as you are going slow enough – and they help the handling at speed – deflecting air around the wheels and tyres. Unfortunately they can also become worn and broken, which usually goes unnoticed.

Fortunately on the 986 they are cheap and easy to replace. If you can use a screwdriver (with selection of Phillips head and torx bits) and on inspection yours are worn or broken, you can replace them.

Drain points are located either side of the battery (top) and (below) on each side of the convertible trim panel

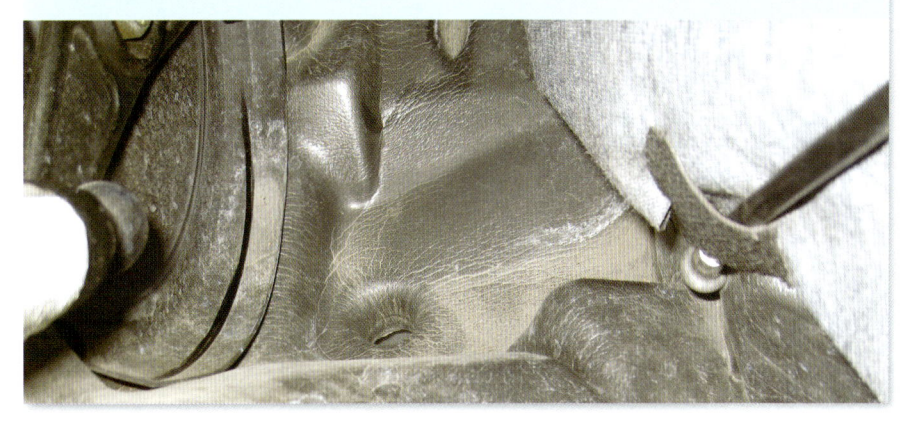

PORSCHE BOXSTER & CAYMAN

These items have been incorporated into the wheel arch liner on the 987, which would mean a hugely increased replacement cost. However I have not heard of the 987 version wearing away so readily. Thankfully they seem to be made of tougher plastic. Incidentally the S also has an additional ¼-cone shaped plastic scoops inboard of these flaps – which are also prone to damage. Likewise they are easily replaced.

Boxster convertible roof

This is an important note for those with a plastic rear screen!

Owners of cars with glass rear windows/screens can skip ahead, but those with plastic rear windows need to take note – the following can save you money and a lot of hassle.

Every winter I get calls from owners of cars with the plastic rear screen who have lowered the roof in cold weather – and it has split across the centre. There are two things to remember to prevent this:

Take note of the passage in the owner's manual that says not to lower the roof in cold weather. Porsche warn the owner – take them seriously!

When you lower the roof at any time, make sure it gently folds horizontally across the middle of the plastic window in an even, rounded, straight line. To do this usually means you have to stop the lowering operation half way through, get out of the car and manually smooth out a couple of little kinks that try to form about ¼ of the way in from each side, before then getting back in and continue lowering the roof.

Yes, this is inconvenient and makes a complete mockery of Porsche's advertising that used to say "the roof can

A set of front wheel lower front flaps and scoops for a 986

58　Ultimate Owners' Guide

The Boxster chop smoothes out kinking in the plastic rear window

be lowered in 12.5 seconds", but it is essential to prevent these kinks forming in to stress-points and eventually, usually on a cold day, the window splits.

This is going to be inconvenient at the best of times, and is awkward and costly to fix. There are roof repair and replacement options (mentioned elsewhere), but prevention is better than cure. Boxster owners have a pet-name for the rear screen's smoothing operation – it is known as 'the Boxster chop'.

Incidentally the need to smooth the kinks out applies equally in the summer. To maintain the window in its best condition you need to smooth out the kinks every time you fold the roof. In addition you really need to make sure there are no bits of grit on the plastic that will grind away between the touching plastic surfaces while you are driving. These will cause the hazing that is all so apparent on some cars. A careful wipe over with a clean duster and if you have

PORSCHE BOXSTER & CAYMAN

it, you can use the 'fleece' (actually a bit of felt-like material that Porsche supply for use when you have the hardtop fitted) placed between the folds of the plastic to prevent scratching. Doing this will prevent such marking and save you having to buy a new rear-window for a long time.

Incidentally if you use a hard top, do remember to clean the plastic window and use the fleece as above, thus avoiding the plastic chafing over the winter months.

"My roof will not go up or down"

Occasionally, the roof will not raise when the button is pressed. There are a few things to check to try and get it working again before heading off to a dealer or specialist. Firstly of course is the handbrake – have you remembered to engage the handbrake? The top will not operate with the handbrake off (unless you have a modified relay – see elsewhere in this book). Next is the fuse – has it blown? As discussed earlier the fuses are located in the driver's footwell and there is a list in the plastic cover showing which fuse protects which functions. Clearly, just replacing a blown fuse may not solve the problem, so you may have to look at the other parts of the roof's electrics.

The next thing to check is the microswitch in the top rail of the windscreen, where the roof locking handle latches. The switch contacts sometimes don't quite operate, and this can often be fixed simply by probing a few times with a finger at the button in the recess where the hook on the operating handle latches.

Sometimes though, the same microswitch may need replacing, or a wire may have become detached. It is not too difficult to get the trim off around this and replace the failed item.

The last thing that can go wrong is the drive to the roof from the motor located at the rear of the roof storage area.

The drive is an electric motor that operates two cables (similar to speedometer cables), one at each side. If one cable breaks this can cause problems if the owner tries to continue to operate

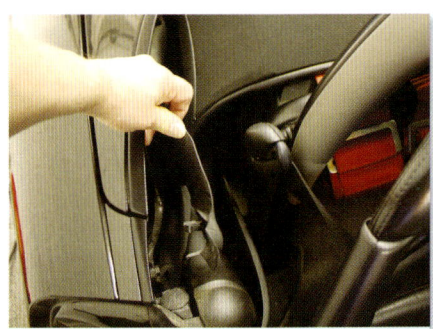

Checking the operation of the microswitch in the top rail of the windscreen

Getting access to the convertible roof drive motor, by unclipping the black cover trim

60 Ultimate Owners' Guide

the roof – the single drive will only raise or lower one side and the frame can be bent or even broken as the resulting twisting force is applied.

Manually raising the roof
Should the roof fail to open and you can't get it to close using the preceding hints, you can manually raise it, but this procedure is a last resort!

You will need the wheel bolt spanner/wrench lever from the tool kit (the long one with a large screwdriver-like blade protected by a plastic cap).

Remove the ignition key.

Unclip the black cover each side of the roof and lift it out.

Take the lever and remove the cap – be careful the blade is ridiculously sharp!

Using the blade of the lever, lever the top ball joints (black) off each side and then the lower red balljoints. Be very careful not to damage the paint or bend the clamshell. The force required to do this can be quite high and you will need to be careful as the connections are under pressure or tension. If the top has failed

Using the wheelbolt wrench sharp end, first (carefully) remove the black balljoints (above), followed by the red balljoints (below)

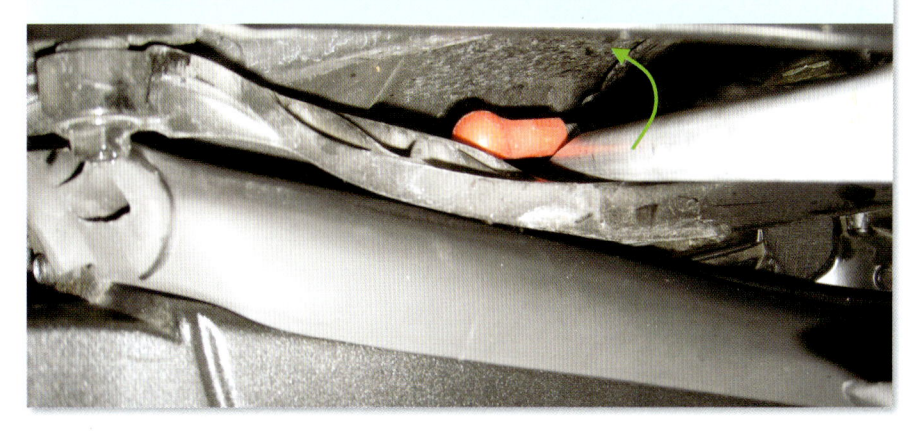

semi-raised, have someone hold the top steady and ready to take the weight to ensure that the roof does not fall down uncontrolled as you lever the final joint apart. The roof is heavy and anything in the way can potentially be damaged or hurt – or that pointed lever might get spun out of your hands.

You can now lift the convertible top from the front centre and latch it in to position as normal.

This will enable you to drive home, or preferably to somewhere to get it fixed. Note that the rear clamshell is no longer locked down, so the car is no longer secure and no wild driving please – as it might flap about.

Roof edge overlaps plastic trim above side window
Sometimes the roof will raise and you will see it has not aligned itself correctly within the plastic trim at the sides of the car. This can usually be fixed by either finding that some Velcro attachments have come undone or that the metal tensioner at the rear of the mechanism has bent

The Velcro straps can be used to adjust the fit of the roof edges at the sides

Sometimes the metal tensioner at the rear of the mechanism has bent too far

too far. You can check the tensioners and compare each side with the other to see how it should work – you can just bend the sprung metal back into position on the offending side.

Plastic window care
The plastic window can accumulate a film over time that makes it almost impossible to see through. Fortunately it is easy to prevent this happening by just giving the plastic a regular clean. Do NOT use any proprietary glass cleaner as some use chemicals that can actually melt, burn, or discolour the plastic – a costly mistake!

Day to day keep the window clean by dusting the window off – especially before lowering the roof. However, every now and again you will need to clean it properly.

Porsche supplied a cleaner with the car when new (and of course this is still available from Porsche parts counters). I used it and found it excellent; people would actually tell me that the window was so clear that they could not tell it was there! However, I find it is not the easiest material to use. It is a white liquid that I feel is fairly aggressive, therefore I only used it about once a year to give the window a really deep clean. It also needs to be kept off the roof material itself – the white will stain the fabric of the roof so be careful not to spill it. Having said that you will almost invariably accidentally stain the piping around the window itself – no matter how careful you are. If this happens you can restore the original look by using a steady hand and a permanent marker. Although a black permanent marker on the black roof will not look right at first, it soon blends in, although I wouldn't want to guarantee it blending in on large areas!

For regular cleaning I use a clear plastic spray-on cleaner such as Novus. This can be sprayed on and wiped off – and the job is done! Very easy to use and can be carried with you to give a quick clean whenever you need it.

So what happens if you bought a car and it has a hazy/fogged/yellow stained window because the previous owner did not bother cleaning it (it happens a lot!)? The Porsche cleaner is a good start if you find it hidden away in the car, or can obtain it from Porsche. An alternative that I have only ever heard good things about is a product called Hindsight (www.hindsightuk.com). This has been used to restore what could well be considered unusable windows to great condition, even reducing scratches and restoring clarity. Another similar product is sold by Renovo (www.renovointernational.com).

Roof material care
The roof itself is 100% Acrylic on the outside (Porsche call it 'Mohair') with a butyl or neoprene waterproof layer, and a cotton liner on the inside. When new the roof is treated to make the outside

Keep the early Boxster's plastic rear window clean and it will last for years

waterproof so that the water beads up. This is not really necessary as the waterproof lining makes sure that water will not permeate the material – even if the outer is soaked. However the external waterproof treatment does not last long – especially if you use car wash on the fabric, in fact mine lasted as long as the first service wash that my dealership gave the car (which I had not asked for). After that the water no longer beaded on the roof.

If you do want the water to bead again 'like new', you can easily reproof the fabric. Porsche make a treatment to do this, however I found it very disappointing. Proprietary proofers like 3M Scotchguard Fabric Protector are popular with owners and easily obtained from DIY or outdoor activity shops.

If you are reproofing the roof then it is prudent not to get the proofer on the plastic window (or other parts) or the paintwork. If it is a spray then this appears to be difficult, but there is a quick and easy way to mask up the car.

An aftermarket glass rear window on my car, described on the following page (above) A misaligned roof edge overlapping the plastic side trim (below left and page 62). Cleaning dried contamination with a fluff remover (below, right)

Firstly, buy a cheap plastic decorator sheet (sorry – you've got to go back to the DIY store again!). Open the roof part way, make a slit in the opened decorator's sheet about one third to one half way along it and feed the sheet over the roof and under the back. Close the roof again trapping the decorator's sheet under the roof, but covering the glass/paintwork/clamshell. Now you just need to mask off the rear window and the plastic trim at the sides of the roof and you have done. Now you can spray the proofer over the roof without worrying.

Glass rear window

There's not much you can say about the glass rear window fitted to 2003MY onwards cars. It has the advantage of not needing the special maintenance that the plastic window requires, is heated so is more usable in winter, can be lowered at any temperature and most importantly, you don't have to get out and do the 'Boxster chop'!

Replacement roof and retrofit glass window.

There will likely come a time when either the roof material and/or the (plastic) window are looking too tired and in need of replacement. Porsche themselves offer a replacement roof only (consisting of the roof material and window), however if it is just the plastic window that requires replacement, there are specialist trimmers who can sew a new window in to your existing roof.

The roof frame is a complex mechanism

Ultimate Owners' Guide

PORSCHE BOXSTER & CAYMAN

An alternative method is a retrofit glass-windowed roof. A burgeoning market has emerged in the last few years, with companies offering a replacement roof complete with glass rear window that is able to be retrofitted to the plastic window models. It is worth noting that the original Porsche glass-windowed roof as fitted to 2003 MY cars will not fit to the earlier (plastic window) cars without replacing not just the roof material, but indeed the whole roof frame and even the side windows. That would be a very expensive way to get a glass window!

However the aftermarket specialists have developed various glass window solutions that do work very well and are, comparatively, reasonably priced – even with fitting. The difference they make to the usability of the folding roof makes them well worth considering when it comes to the time to renew the window or roof.

Among those that offer these glass/fabric replacement roofs are: BAS International (www.car-hood.co.uk) and GAHH (www.gahh.com).

Windstop (Boxster only!)

A common complaint is that the windstop in the centre of the roll-over bar is rattling or even that "it doesn't stay in over 70mph" – quite wrong!

Either of these cases actually indicates it is not fitted correctly. Usually you will need to remove the windstop periodically to enable access to the rear window for cleaning – or if you want that real 'wind in the hair' feeling now and again!

It is actually very simple to remove and replace, but so easy to get wrong. Start at one side, apply a slight downward pressure with one hand to the one side, whilst pushing the latch behind the windstop gently towards the centre of the car just a few mm (no more than about 1/8th inch for those used to imperial measurements). Then while keeping the downward pressure and holding the latch open, slide that side of the windstop towards the rear of the car. It will unhook from the fixing on the roll-over bar and then you can just repeat with the other side and remove it – the other side will be much easier.

While you have the windstop removed take a look at the latches. If you look through the windstop at the latches, and move them over as if you were unlatching them you will see a small red dot on the back of the latch (on early latches only). This can help when you reinstall the windstop.

Note the latches are fragile. If you can see all of the red dot through the windstop then you have moved it far enough over to be able to remove and install. If you do not have the red dot, there is no need to move the latch more than shown in the accompanying photo.

To replace the windstop just reverse the above. Start by inserting the windstop from the rear. Locate the centre against the stop at the bottom of the roll-over bar and put the windstop up against the rear of the rollbar. Push down and slide in one side, then the other. The latches will sort themselves out this time. After you have replaced the windstop look through it at the latch area. If you can see the red dots, the latches are not located properly and the windstop will rattle or could even fall

PORSCHE BOXSTER & CAYMAN

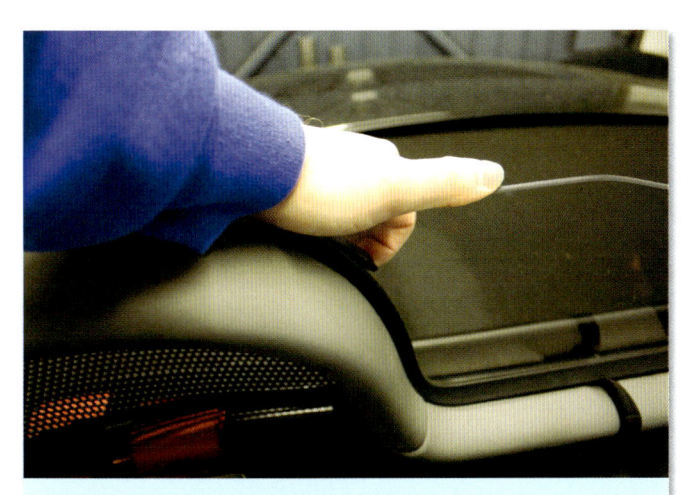

You only remove the windstop latches this far

To refit, locate the centre at the base of the roll-over bar

out. If you have no red dot, the latches should not be over the plexiglass. You can also ensure the windstop is located correctly by gently shaking the top of each side – it should not come loose.

To clean the windstop use something suitable for cleaning plastics. Motor-cycle helmet visor cleaner or the previously mentioned Novus is ideal as it will not damage the plastic. DO NOT use the white Porsche cleaner supplied for the plastic rear window on the windstop – it could damage the clarity.

If the latches have broken on your windstop then replacements are available at quite reasonable price from Porsche. The part numbers (at time of writing) are: 986-561-323-00

Incidentally, Can it fall out over 70mph? Definitely not! The wind is coming from behind you as it gets sucked back in to the open car as you drive. As the windstop is fitted from the rear, the wind coming from behind you actually pushes the windstop against its mounting points and makes it more secure, not less. I have personally had the car up to 150mph several times on the German autobahns with the top down – and I've still got the same windstop that my car came with.

Ultimate Owners' Guide **67**

Enhancements and updates

An easy way to update the look of pre-2003 cars is to use the clear rear lights from the 2003 MY car as detailed in the Electrics section. However, you can also fit the later front and rear bumper covers to complete the look. Alternatively any of the various aerokits that Porsche have offered over the years can be fitted to the appropriate body design (unfortunately you can't fit 986 kits to 987 and vice-versa). There is no actual bodywork modification required, all the parts just bolt on, so it is a reasonably easy and effective way to freshen the look of your car if you feel the need for change.

The 987 and Cayman models can likewise be fitted with the larger rear extending spoilers, rear bumper with diffuser and the front spoiler lips of the Sport Edition models.

It should be noted that changing just the front or back individually should not be contemplated. (It is specifically warned against by Porsche). The elements are designed to work together to maintain the overall aerodynamic balance of the car. Adding (for example) just the rear spoiler wing of the 986 aerokit 2 without the corresponding

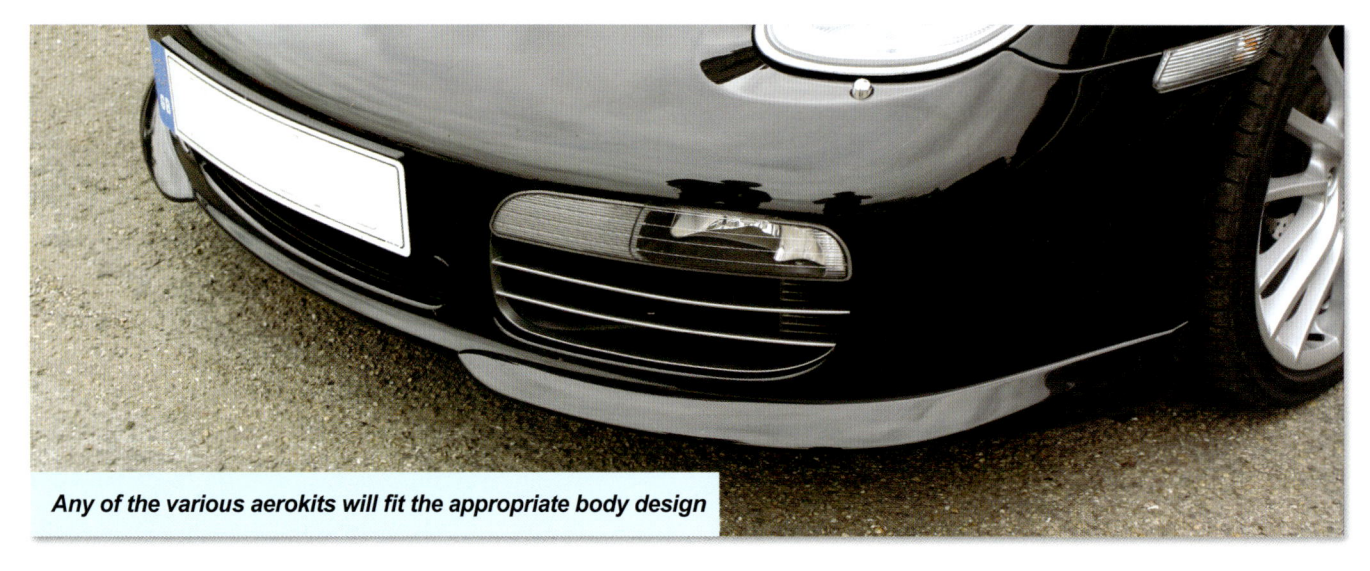

Any of the various aerokits will fit the appropriate body design

extended front bumper spoiler could prove dangerous at high speeds.

Car Body Care

You may ask why there is a section telling you how to wash the car. If this is telling you the obvious, I won't insult you by telling you what to do and please do skip ahead. For anyone else who may be interested, here is how I care for my car.

Washing the bodywork

Before you start, raise the rear spoiler using the switch on the fuse panel in the footwell.

I start by cleaning the wheels using a non-acid wheel cleaner such as P21S (now known as R222 in Europe). I spray the wheels with the cleaner first, and then use a wheel brush and a thin washing-up sponge to get in to all the nooks and crannies. Ensure that the inside of the wheels, behind the spokes etc are all cleaned, and don't forget the brake calipers.

Rinse the wheels off. Then, as long as the exhaust is cool, I clean the exhaust box and tips using P21S polishing soap. This is an incredibly easy way to clean the exhaust (which on many Boxsters IS visible from behind the car), and much quicker and easier than traditional metal polish pastes. Rinse the exhaust off and wipe to remove any residue.

Rinse the car with a hose. Then use a pressure washer fitted with an application lance (taking care not to squirt water into the exhaust outlet) I use Snow foam to soak off any persistent dirt (this is the only part that requires anything out of the ordinary – you can skip it if you prefer, but it does help lift and soften any baked on grime).

Note: Do not use the snow foam or car wash on the soft top. It will remove the waterproofing. To clean the top you can normally just rinse it with clear water from the hose and it will come up fine.

Allow the snow foam to work for 5 to 10 minutes and rinse off.

Use a non-acid wheel cleaner followed by a wheel brush and a thin washing up sponge

I clean the exhaust and tips using P21S polishing soap. The exhaust is visible on many Boxsters!

PORSCHE BOXSTER & CAYMAN

Whist the snow foam is working you might want to hose and wash under the wheel arches – make sure you get into areas such as the return flange on the wheelarch edge itself – mud and dirt that accumulates in traps such as this can cause corrosion later in any car's life. Use a separate brush to clean these underbody areas – **not** the wash-mitt you are planning to use on the paintwork!

After this it is out with the buckets – one for the car wash and one with clear water to rinse the wash mitt – wool or microfibre types are both good. Never use a sponge as it will hold all the tiny grit and dirt particles and these will scratch the paintwork.

Load the wash-mitt up from the first bucket, apply to the car and when you need to reload the mitt with more car wash, RINSE it first in the clear-water bucket. This will keep most of the dirt and grit in the bottom of the rinse bucket, rather than applying it all over again to the next part of the car.

Start at the upper surfaces of the car and work your way around, one panel at a time, washing the top half of the car before the lower. When applying the wash mitt to the paint move it in straight lines – moving around in circles will result in that horrid swirl effect in the paint.

I try to wash front to back for the horizontal surfaces and up and down for the vertical ones. After all the preparation and rinsing this should be a quick stage – all that is being removed is the persistent layer of road film that is stuck to the car – all the heavy stuff will have been softened and rinsed off already by the snow foam.

Rinse again. At the end of the rinse process try holding the hose close to the paintwork using a very low flow rate, this will allow most of the water to sheet off the panel and you will not get thousands of water droplets on the paint as you would when you spray the car.

Finally, to dry the car I use a waffle-weave microfiber drying towel. To aid drying and help prevent any remaining water spots I use a spritz of instant-detailer spray on each panel. The instant-detailer acts as a drying aid – breaking the surface tension on the water drops, and helps top up the shine. A final wipe over with a microfiber polishing cloth will bring up the final finish.

After drying the exterior, open the roof a small amount and dry under the clamshell. There are some channels at the sides that can be water traps and it is useful to dry these out as a preventative measure against corrosion. Dry along the top of the windscreen rail (where the roof butts up against it) and wipe along the corresponding rubber edge of the roof. This will keep it clear of debris, which could allow water to get in to the car if it rains.

I also open all the doors and luggage compartments and dry around the channels in there, and the underneath of the panels where they are exposed to the water. Dry the door jambs and make sure that there is no dirt trapped

70   Ultimate Owners' Guide

that could be a corrosion trap.

Lastly, to ensure the brakes do not get corroded with all the water that has been sprayed into them, I highly recommend taking the car for a short drive (long enough for the engine to warm up is a good idea). The water that will have got in to the brakes will be spun out and braking hard a few times will generate enough heat to make sure the discs are fully dried out. Doing this one simple thing can help prevent getting a huge bill to replace the brakes because they have been left to sit with water in them after washing.

Every few months it is advisable to protect the paintwork using a good wax or a sealant. You can polish before waxing but don't confuse the two. Polish is used to smooth the paint and takes a minute layer of paint (or clear-coat) off. It will expose the fresh paint and leave it exposed. If you polish, then you must follow up with either a wax or a polymer sealant in order to protect the paint.

Car care is a subject that can fill a book on its own, so the above is just a guide to basic care of the bodywork and is suitable for most who want to keep their car looking good day to day. For those that wish to maintain that better-than-showroom shine, or enter concours competitions, there is a lot more information that can be found.

At this time website forums such as www.autopia.org/forum, www.detailingworld.co.uk/forum/ and www.cleanyourcar.co.uk/forum/ are excellent sources of information.

Protect the paint every few months with a wax or polymer sealant. This is my car, still looking good after 9 years

Ultimate Owners' Guide

MAINTENANCE SCHEDULES

Porsche have revised the requirements and frequency of the official maintenance schedule repeatedly over the time the car has been in production, and it depends on which model year you have as to the actual schedule that you should be following - sometimes Official Porsche Centres themselves seem a little confused as to what should be done and when! Actually, they are more often very sure of what should be done and when, but what they say occasionally doesn't tally with the information that Porsche give in the service and maintenance book… It can be useful for the owner to know the correct schedule in order to avoid unnecessary, and costly, extra work being done.

It is highly recommended that the specified service schedule appropriate for your particular year and model is followed as a minimum. Note that the following maintenance schedules are divided into recommendations for USA models and RoW models (where RoW is an abbreviation for Rest of the World models).

It is important to follow the appropriate service schedule for your model

72 Ultimate Owners' Guide

US up to 2004 MY Maintenance Schedules

MAINTENANCE TYPE	US cars up to MY 2002 Annual Check — Cars with annual mileages of less than 9,000 miles*	US cars up to MY 2002 Minor — 15,000, 45,000, 75,000, 105,000 miles etc	US cars up to MY 2002 Major — 30,000, 60,000, 90,000, 120,000 miles etc	US cars MY 2003 Annual Check — Cars with annual mileages of less than 9,000 miles*	US cars MY 2003 Minor — 15,000, 45,000, 75,000, 105,000 miles etc	US cars MY 2003 Major — 30,000, 60,000, 90,000, 120,000 miles etc	US cars MY 2004 Annual Check — No Annual check for MY04 onwards	US cars MY 2004 Minor — 15,000, 45,000, 75,000, 105,000 miles etc	US cars MY 2004 Major — 30,000, 60,000, 90,000, 120,000 miles etc
Diagnosis system: Read out fault memory	X	X	X	X	X	X		X	X
Polyrib belt: Check condition			X			X			X
Engine: Check oil level	X								
Change the engine oil		X		X	X			X	
Change the engine oil and oil filter			X			X			X
Replace the spark plugs			X			X			X
Vehicle underside and engine compartment: Visual inspection for leaks (oils and fluids) and abrasion (lines and hoses) Underbody panels: visual inspection for completeness, installation and damage	X	X	X	X	X	X		X	X
Power steering: Check the fluid level and bellows	X	X		X	X			X	
Coolant hoses: Check condition;		X	X		X	X		X	X
Radiators and air inlets at front: Visual inspection for external contamination and blockage;	X	X	X	X	X	X		X	X
Coolant: Check the level and antifreeze protection			X		X	X		X	X

Ultimate Owners' Guide

PORSCHE BOXSTER & CAYMAN

US up to 2004 MY *Continued...*	US cars up to MY 2002			US cars MY 2003			US cars MY 2004		
	Annual Check	Minor	Major	Annual Check	Minor	Major	Annual Check	Minor	Major
Air cleaner: Replace the filter element			X			X			X
Particle filter: Replace the filter element		X	X		X	X		X	X
Fuel system: Visual inspection for damage, routing and secure fit of line connections			X			X			X
Power steering: Check the fluid level and bellows			X			X			X
Parking brake: Checking the free play of the parking brake lever			X			X			X
Brake system: Visual inspection of the brake pads and brake discs for wear			X			X			X
Brake hoses and lines: Visual inspection for damage, routing and corrosion. Checking the brake fluid level	X	X	X	X	X	X		X	X
Clutch: Check the play & pedal end position			X			X			X
Throttle actuation: Check smooth operation, check the full throttle position with the Tester			X						
Steering gear: Visually inspect the bellows for damage	X		X	X		X			X
Tie rod joints: Check the play & dust bellows	X		X	X		X			X
Axle joints: Check play, visual inspection of dust bellows for damage, check screw connections of running gear adjustment facility, front and rear, for secure fit	X		X	X		X			X

74 Ultimate Owners' Guide

PORSCHE BOXSTER & CAYMAN

US up to 2004 MY *Continued...*	US cars up to MY 2002 Annual Check	Minor	Major	US cars MY 2003 Annual Check	Minor	Major	US cars MY 2004 Annual Check	Minor	Major
Drive shafts: Perform a visual inspection of the boots for leaks and damage	X	X	X	X	X	X		X	X
Exhaust system: Visual inspection for leaks and damage, check suspension			X			X			X
Tires and spare wheel (collapsible wheel): Check the condition and the tire pressure	X	X	X	X	X	X		X	X
Check the door locks, lid locks and safety hooks of the front lid to ensure that they are secure and functioning properly: Check lid lock, front and rear; Check safety hook, front lid; Function test, check door lock; Check door and lid tightening torques; Check inner release of luggage compartment (Trunk Entrapment)		X	X		X	X		X	X
Seat belts: Check function and condition			X			X			X
Vehicle lighting: Check function; All headlights: Check adjustment; Horn: Check operation.	X	X	X	X	X	X		X	X
Windscreen wiper/washer system, headlight washer: Check fluid level and nozzle settings, pay attention to antifreeze protection in the winter months.		X	X		X	X		X	X

Ultimate Owners' Guide

PORSCHE BOXSTER & CAYMAN

US up to 2004 MY *Continued...*	US cars up to MY 2002			US cars MY 2003			US cars MY 2004		
	Annual Check	Minor	Major	Annual Check	Minor	Major	Annual Check	Minor	Major
Electrical equipment as well as warning and indicator lights: Check operation.	X	X	X	X	X	X		X	X
Test drive:	X	X	X	X	X	X		X	X
Remote control, front seats, foot and parking brakes (also actuation travel), engine, clutch, steering, transmission, ParkAssist, automatic speed control, TC/PSM switch, heating, air-conditioning system and instruments: Check operation.	X	X	X	X	X	X		X	X
Oils, fluids: Visual inspection for leaks	X	X	X	X	X	X		X	X

Minor Maintenance Notes:
It is urgently recommended to check the air cleaner (and replace it if necessary) each time minor maintenance is carried out.

■ On vehicles with annual mileages of less than 9,000 miles (15,000 km), an annual maintenance must be carried out once a year.

■ Maintenance with oil filter change must be carried out at least every 2 years according to the mileage, if the mileage for a major maintenance has not already been reached.

■ For an annual mileage of more than 9,000 miles (15,000 km) it is recommended to carry out the next maintenance as soon as possible.

■ If the mileage for a regular service is not reached, minor maintenance must be carried out after 2, 6, 10 .... years. (MY2004)

■ The term "checking" includes all necessary subsequent work such as adjusting, readjusting, correcting and topping up, but does not include repairing, replacing and reconditioning parts or assemblies.

Test item: Checking inner unlocking of luggage compartment (Trunk Entrapment) has been added to the countries specification CO2 (for USA) and C36 (for Canada) from model year 2003.

Major Maintenance Notes:
The term "checking" includes all

necessary subsequent work such as adjusting, readjusting, correcting and topping up, but does not include repairing, replacing and reconditioning parts or assemblies.

■ The maintenance item Throttle actuation: Check smooth operation, check full throttle position with the Tester is omitted as of model year 2002.

■ The maintenance item Replace the spark plugs depends on the model year. Please see Additional Maintenance

■ The test item Checking inner unlocking of luggage compartment (Trunk Entrapment) has been added to the countries specification CO2 (for USA) and C36 (for Canada) from model year 2003.

■ If the mileage for a regular service is not reached, major maintenance must be carried out after 4,8, 12.... Years (MY2004)

Annual Maintenance Notes:

■ On vehicles with annual mileages of less than 9,000 miles (15,000 km), an annual maintenance must be carried out once a year.

■ Maintenance with oil filter change must be carried out at least every 2 years according to the mileage, if the mileage for a major maintenance has not already been reached.

■ For an annual mileage of more than 9,000 miles (15,000 km) it is recommended to carry out the next maintenance as soon as possible.

■ The term "checking" includes all necessary subsequent work such as adjusting, readjusting, correcting and topping up, but does not include repairing, replacing and reconditioning parts or assemblies.

Additional maintenance, replacing spark plugs

Up to and including MY99 every 30,000 miles (48,000 km)

As of MY01 every 60,000 miles (96,000 km) or at least every 4 years

Additional maintenance every 60,000 miles (96,000 km)

Important Note: It is recommended to replace the fuel filter every 60,000 miles (96,000 km) up to and including MY01.
Replace Polyrib belt

Additional maintenance every 90,000 miles (144,000 km)

Manual transmission: - Changing transmission oil
Automatic transmission:
Replace ATF
Replace ATF filter
Change transmission oil in final drive

Maintenance every 2 years

Change brake fluid (use only original Porsche brake fluid)
Condition report - preparing long-life guarantee

Maintenance after 4, 8, 10 then every 2 years

Inspect air bag system
Mounting of assemblies and running gear: Visual inspection of all rubber mounts for damage.

PORSCHE BOXSTER & CAYMAN

RoW cars up to MY 2002 Maintenance Schedules

MAINTENANCE TYPE	RoW cars up to MY 2002 – Annual Check (Cars with annual mileages of less than 9,000 miles*)	RoW cars up to MY 2002 – Minor (12,000, 36,000, 60,000, 34,000 miles etc)	RoW cars up to MY 2002 – Major (24,000, 48,000, 72,000, 96,000 miles, etc)	RoW cars MY 2003 – Annual Check (Cars with annual mileages of less than 9,000 miles*)	RoW cars MY 2003 – Minor (12,000, 36,000, 60,000, 34,000 miles etc)	RoW cars MY 2003 – Major (24,000, 48,000, 72,000, 96,000 miles, etc)	RoW cars MY 2004 – Annual Check (No annual check for MY04 onwards)	RoW cars MY 2004 – Minor (12,000, 36,000, 60,000, 34,000 miles etc)	RoW cars MY 2004 – Major (24,000, 48,000, 72,000, 96,000 miles, etc)
Diagnosis system: Read out fault memory	X	X	X	X	X	X		X	X
Polyrib belt: Check condition			X			X			X
Engine: Check oil level	X								
Change the engine oil		X		X	X			X	
Change the engine oil and oil filter			X			X			X
Replace the spark plugs			X			X			X
Vehicle underside and engine compartment: Visual inspection for leaks (oils & fluids) and abrasion (lines & hoses) Underbody panels: visual inspection for completeness, installation and damage	X	X	X	X	X	X		X	X
Power steering: Check the fluid level & bellows	X	X		X	X			X	
Coolant hoses: Check condition;		X	X		X	X		X	X
Radiators and air inlets at front: Visual inspection for external contamination and blockage;	X	X	X	X	X	X		X	X
Coolant: Check the level and antifreeze protection			X		X	X		X	X

PORSCHE BOXSTER & CAYMAN

RoW cars up to MY 2002 *Continued....*	RoW cars up to MY 2002			RoW cars MY 2003			RoW cars MY 2004		
	Annual Check	Minor	Major	Annual Check	Minor	Major	Annual Check	Minor	Major
Air cleaner: Replace the filter element			X			X			X
Particle filter: Replace the filter element		X	X		X	X		X	X
Fuel system: Visual inspection for damage, routing and secure fit of line connections			X			X			X
Power steering: Check the fluid level and bellows			X			X			X
Parking brake: Checking the free play of the parking brake lever			X			X			X
Brake system: Visual inspection of the brake pads and brake discs for wear			X			X			X
Brake hoses and lines: Visual inspection for damage, routing and corrosion. Checking the brake fluid level	X	X	X	X	X	X		X	X
Clutch: Check the play and pedal end position			X			X			X
Throttle actuation: Check smooth operation, check the full throttle position with the Tester			X						
Steering gear: Visually inspect the bellows for damage	X		X	X		X			X
Tie rod joints: Check the play & dust bellows	X		X	X		X			X
Axle joints: Check play, visual inspection of dust bellows for damage, check screw connections of running gear adjustment facility, front and rear, for secure fit	X		X	X		X			X

Ultimate Owners' Guide   79

PORSCHE BOXSTER & CAYMAN

RoW cars up to MY 2002 Continued....	RoW cars up to MY 2002			RoW cars MY 2003			RoW cars MY 2004		
	Annual Check	Minor	Major	Annual Check	Minor	Major	Annual Check	Minor	Major
Drive shafts: Perform a visual inspection of the boots for leaks and damage	X	X	X	X	X	X		X	X
Exhaust system: Visual inspection for leaks and damage, check suspension			X			X			X
Tires and spare wheel (collapsible wheel): Check the condition and the tire pressure	X	X	X	X	X	X		X	X
Check the door locks, lid locks and safety hooks of the front lid to ensure that they are secure and functioning properly: Check lid lock, front and rear; Check safety hook, front lid; Function test, check door lock; Check door and lid tightening torques		X	X		X	X		X	X
Seat belts: Check function and condition			X			X			X
Vehicle lighting: Check function; All headlights: Check adjustment; Horn: Check operation.	X	X	X	X	X	X		X	X
Windscreen wiper/washer system, headlight washer: Check fluid level and nozzle settings, pay attention to antifreeze protection in the winter months.		X	X		X	X		X	X
Electrical equipment as well as warning and indicator lights: Check operation.	X	X	X	X	X	X		X	X
Test drive:	X	X	X	X	X	X		X	X

PORSCHE BOXSTER & CAYMAN

RoW cars up to MY 2002 Continued....	RoW cars up to MY 2002			RoW cars MY 2003			RoW cars MY 2004		
	Annual Check	Minor	Major	Annual Check	Minor	Major	Annual Check	Minor	Major
Remote control, front seats, foot and parking brakes (also actuation travel), engine, clutch, steering, transmission, ParkAssist, automatic speed control, TC/PSM switch, heating, air-conditioning system and instruments: Check operation.	X	X	X	X	X	X		X	X
Oils, fluids: Visual inspection for leaks	X	X	X	X	X	X		X	X

Minor Maintenance Notes:
Important Notes:
- Not valid for USA!
- The engine oil and oil filter must be changed every 10,000 km (6,000 miles) on vehicles which are operated in countries with leaded fuel (country coding M 150 in the control unit).
- On vehicles with annual mileages of less than 15,000 km (9,000 miles), an annual maintenance must be carried out once a year.
- Maintenance with oil filter change must be carried out at least every 2 years according to the mileage, if the mileage for a major maintenance has not already been reached.
- For an annual mileage of more than 15,000 km (9,000 miles) it is recommended to carry out the next maintenance as soon as possible.
- The term "checking" includes all necessary subsequent work such as adjusting, readjusting, correcting and topping up, but does not include repairing, replacing and reconditioning parts or assemblies.
- The test item Checking inner unlocking of luggage compartment (Trunk Entrapment) has been added to the countries specification CO2 (for USA) and C36 (for Canada) from model year 2003.
- The maintenance item Replace the spark plugs depends on the model year. Please see Additional Maintenance

Major Maintenance Notes:
- Not valid for USA.
- The engine oil and oil filter must be changed every 10,000 km (6,000

Ultimate Owners' Guide

PORSCHE BOXSTER & CAYMAN

miles) on vehicles which are operated in countries with leaded fuel (country coding M 150 in the control unit).

■ The term "checking" includes all necessary subsequent work such as adjusting, readjusting, correcting and topping up, but does not include repairing, replacing and reconditioning parts or assemblies.

■ The maintenance item Throttle actuation: Check smooth operation, check full throttle position with the Tester omitted as of model year 2002.

■ The maintenance item Replace the spark plugs depends on the model year. Please see Additional Maintenance

Annual Maintenance Notes:
Note - Covers all years up to MY03
 ■ Not valid for USA!
 ■ The engine oil and oil filter must be changed every 10,000 km (6,000 miles) on vehicles which are operated in countries with leaded fuel (country coding M 150 in the control unit).
 ■ On vehicles with annual mileages of less than 15,000 km (9,000 miles),

an annual maintenance must be carried out once a year.
 ■ Maintenance with oil filter change must be carried out at least every 2 years according to the mileage, if the mileage for a major maintenance has not already been reached.
 ■ The term "checking" includes all necessary subsequent work such as adjusting, readjusting, correcting and topping up, but does not include repairing, replacing and reconditioning parts or assemblies.

Additional maintenance, replacing spark plugs
Up to and including MY99 every 40,000 Km
MY00 every 60,000 Km
As of MY01 every 48,000 miles (80,000 Km), at least every 4 years

Additional maintenance every 48,000 miles (80,000 km)
Replace the fuel filter up to and including MY01.
Replace Polyrib belt

Additional maintenance every 96,000 miles (160,000 km)
Manual transmission: - Changing transmission oil
Automatic transmission:
Replace ATF
Replace ATF filter
Change transmission oil in final drive

Maintenance every 2 years
Change brake fluid (use only original Porsche brake fluid)
Condition report - preparing long-life guarantee

Maintenance after 4, 8, 10 then every 2 years
Inspect air bag system
Mounting of assemblies and running gear: Visual inspection of all rubber mounts for damage
Note:
 ■ The engine oil and oil filter must be changed every 10,000 km (6,000 miles) on vehicles which are operated in countries with leaded fuel (country coding M 150 in the control unit).

PORSCHE BOXSTER & CAYMAN

US 987 Maintenance Schedules

MAINTENANCE TYPE	US cars MY 2005-2007 Minor — 20,000, 60,000, 100,000, 140,000 miles etc.	US cars MY 2005-2007 Major — 40,000, 80,000, 120,000, 160,000 miles etc.	US cars MY 2008 Minor — 24,000, 60,000, 96,000, 132,000 miles etc	US cars MY 2008 Major — 36,000, 72,000, 108,000, 144,000 miles etc	US cars MY 2009 Intermediate — 20,000, 60,000, 100,000, 140,000 miles etc.	US cars MY 2009 Major — 40,000, 80,000, 120,000, 180,000 miles etc.
Diagnosis system: Read fault memory; reset maintenance interval/Read and record range information on R.O.	X	X	X	X	X	X
Change engine oil and oil filter	X	X	X	X		
Change engine oil and oil filter (Every 10,000 miles/15,000 km, see separate Oil Change Sheet, PNA 000 162 EF)					X	X
Vehicle underside and engine compartment: Visual inspection for leaks (oils and fluids) and abrasion (lines and hoses); Underbody panels: visual inspection for completeness, installation and damage		X		X	X	X
Coolant hoses: Check condition / Radiators and air intakes: Visual inspection for external debris and blockage / Coolant: Check level and antifreeze protection level	X	X	X	X	X	X
Air filter: Check the air filter condition, and if necessary, replace	X					
Air filter: Replace filter element		X		X		X
Pollen filter: Replace filter element	X	X		X	X	X
Fuel lines & connections: Visual inspection for damage & leaks		X		X		X
Brake system: Visual inspection of the brake pads and brake discs for wear	X	X	X	X	X	X
Parking brake: Check free play of parking brake lever		X		X		X

Ultimate Owners' Guide

PORSCHE BOXSTER & CAYMAN

US 987 Continued...	US cars MY 2005-2007 Minor	US cars MY 2005-2007 Major	US cars MY 2008 Minor	US cars MY 2008 Major	US cars MY 2009 Intermediate	US cars MY 2009 Major
Brake hoses and lines: Visual inspection for damage, routing and corrosion	X	X		X	X	X
Clutch: Check the pedal play and dust boots		X				
Steering gear: Visual inspection of the dust boots for damage Tie rod ends: Check play and dust boots		X		X		X
Axle joints: Check play; visual inspection of the dust boots for damage. Check the screw connections of the front and rear running gear adjustment points are secure		X		X		X
Drive shafts: Visual inspection of the dust boots for leaks and damage	X	X		X	X	X
Exhaust system: Visual inspection for leaks and damage; check mounting and heat shields		X		X		X
Tires: Check condition and tire pressure	X	X	X	X	X	X
Check firewall and cabrio section body drains for debris	X	X	X	X	X	X
Check the door, lid locks and safety hook of the front lid for secure seating and function properly	X	X	X	X	X	X
Seat belts: Check function and condition		X		X		X
Vehicle lighting: Check function All headlights: Check setting	X	X		X	X	X
Horn: Check function	X	X		X	X	X
Windshield wiper/washer system, headlight washer: Check fluid level and nozzle settings (use winter antifreeze protection during winter months)	X	X		X	X	X
Check wiper blades					X	X
Battery: Check condition and electrolyte level	X	X	X	X	X	X

PORSCHE BOXSTER & CAYMAN

US 987 Continued...	US cars MY 2005-2007 Minor	US cars MY 2005-2007 Major	US cars MY 2008 Minor	US cars MY 2008 Major	US cars MY 2009 Intermediate	US cars MY 2009 Major
Electrical equipment, warning and indicator lights: Check function	X	X	X	X	X	X
Additional maintenance for spark plugs						
Replace spark plugs every 60,000 miles (90,000 km) or every 4 years	X	X				
Replace spark plugs every 36,000 miles (60,000 km) or every 4 years			X	X		
Replace spark plugs every 40,000 miles (60,000 km) or every 4 years					X	X
Additional maintenance for drive belt						
Check drive belt at 36,000 miles (60,000 km) or every 4 years			X	X		
Check drive belt at 84,000 miles (140,000 km) or every 10 years			X	X		
Check drive belt at 132,000 miles (220,000 km) or every 16 years			X	X		
Check drive belt at 40,000 miles (60,000 km) or every 4 years	X	X			X	X
Check drive belt at 100,000 miles (150,000 km) or every 10 years	X	X			X	X
Check drive belt at 160,000 miles (240,000 km) or every 16 years	X	X			X	X
Additional maintenance for convertible top						
Maintain and care for convertible top at 12,000 miles (20,000 km) or every 2 years			X	X		
Maintain and care for convertible top at 20,000 miles (30,000 km) or every 2 years	X	X			X	X

Ultimate Owners' Guide

PORSCHE BOXSTER & CAYMAN

US 987 Continued...	US cars MY 2005-2007 Minor	US cars MY 2005-2007 Major	US cars MY 2008 Minor	US cars MY 2008 Major	US cars MY 2009 Intermediate	US cars MY 2009 Major
Additional maintenance 60,000 miles (90,000 km) or every 6 years						
Replace drive belt	X	X	X	X	X	X
PDK Change clutch oil					X	X
Additional maintenance every 108,000 miles (180,000 km) or 12 years						
Change manual transmission oil			X	X		
Change Tiptronic transmission oil and ATF filter			X	X		
Change Tiptronic transmission final drive oil			X	X		
Additional maintenance every 120,000 miles (180,000 km) or 12 years						
Change manual transmission oil	X	X			X	X
Change Tiptronic transmission oil and ATF filter	X	X				
Change Tiptronic transmission final drive oil	X	X				
Change PDK transmission oil					X	X
Every 2 years						
Change brake fluid	X	X	X	X	X	X
File Condition Report for Long-Life guarantee	X	X	X	X		
Every 4 years						
Replace tire sealant	X	X	X	X	X	X
After 4, then every 2 years						
Check battery for the tire pressure monitoring system	X	X	X	X	X	X

PORSCHE BOXSTER & CAYMAN

US 987 *Continued...*	US cars MY 2005-2007		US cars MY 2008		US cars MY 2009	
	Minor	Major	Minor	Major	Intermediate	Major
After 4, 8, 10, then every 2 years						
Inspect airbag system	X	X	X	X	X	X
Assembly and running gear mounts: Visual inspection of all rubber/hydraulic mounts for damage	X	X	X	X	X	X
Road Test Check						
Remote control, front seats, foot brake and parking brake (also operating travel), engine, clutch, steering, transmission, ParkAssist, automatic speed control, PSM switch, PASM switch, Sport switch, heater, air-conditioning system and instruments: Check operation	X	X	X	X	X	X
Oils, fluids: Visual inspection for leaks	X	X	X	X	X	X
NOTES						
Note: If the mileage for scheduled minor maintenance is not reached, Minor maintenance must be performed no later than after 2, 6, 10..... years.	X				X	
Note: If the mileage for scheduled minor/intermediate maintenance is not reached, Minor/intermediate maintenance must be performed no later than after 2, 5, 8, 11..... years.			X			X
Note: If the mileage for scheduled major maintenance is not reached, Major maintenance must be performed no later than after 3, 6, 9, 12..... years.				X		
Note: If the mileage for scheduled major maintenance is not reached, Major maintenance must be performed no later than after 4, 8, 12..... years.		X				X

The terms 'check' and 'inspection' include all necessary subsequent work such as adjusting, readjusting, correcting and topping off, but do not include repairing, replacing and reconditioning parts or assemblies.

Ultimate Owners' Guide

PORSCHE BOXSTER & CAYMAN

ROW 987 Maintenance Schedules

	RoW cars MY 2005-2007		RoW cars MY 2008 0n	
	Minor	Major	Minor	Major
MAINTENANCE TYPE	Every 20,000 miles or 2 years.	Every 40,000 miles or 4 years.	Every 20,000 miles or 2 years.	Every 40,000 miles or 4 years.
Diagnosis system: Read fault memory; reset maintenance interval/Read and record range information on R.O.	X	X	X	X
Change engine oil and oil filter	X	X	X	X
Change engine oil and oil filter (Every 10,000 miles/15,000 km, see separate Oil Change Sheet, PNA 000 162 EF)				
Vehicle underside and engine compartment: Visual inspection for leaks (oils and fluids) and abrasion (lines and hoses); Underbody panels: visual inspection for completeness, installation and damage		X		X
Coolant hoses: Check condition Radiators and air intakes: Visual inspection for external debris and blockage Coolant: Check level and antifreeze protection level	X	X	X	X
Air filter: Check the air filter condition, and if necessary, replace	X			
Air filter: Replace filter element		X		X
Pollen filter: Replace filter element	X	X		X
Fuel lines and connections: Visual inspection for damage and leaks		X		X
Brake system: Visual inspection of the brake pads and brake discs for wear	X	X	X	X
Parking brake: Check free play of parking brake lever		X		X
Brake hoses and lines: Visual inspection for damage, routing and corrosion	X	X		X
Clutch: Check the pedal play and dust boots		X		
Steering gear: Visual inspection of the dust boots for damage Tie rod ends: Check play and dust boots		X		X

PORSCHE BOXSTER & CAYMAN

ROW 987 Continued...	RoW cars MY 2005-2007		RoW cars MY 2008 0n	
	Minor	Major	Minor	Major
Axle joints: Check play; visual inspection of the dust boots for damage. Check the screw connections of the front and rear running gear adjustment points are secure		X		X
Drive shafts: Visual inspection of the dust boots for leaks and damage	X	X		X
Exhaust system: Visual inspection for leaks and damage; check mounting and heat shields		X		X
Tires: Check condition and tire pressure	X	X	X	X
Check firewall and cabrio section body drains for debris	X	X	X	X
Check the door, lid locks and safety hook of the front lid for secure seating and function properly	X	X	X	X
Seat belts: Check function and condition		X		X
Vehicle lighting: Check function All headlights: Check setting	X	X		X
Horn: Check function	X	X		X
Windshield wiper/washer system, headlight washer: Check fluid level and nozzle settings (use winter antifreeze protection during winter months)	X	X		X
Check wiper blades				
Battery: Check condition and electrolyte level	X	X	X	X
Electrical equipment, warning and indicator lights: Check function	X	X	X	X
Additional maintenance for spark plugs				
Replace spark plugs every 60,000 miles (90,000 km) or every 4 years	X	X		
Replace spark plugs every 36,000 miles (60,000 km) or every 4 years			X	X
Replace spark plugs every 40,000 miles (60,000 km) or every 4 years				

Ultimate Owners' Guide

PORSCHE BOXSTER & CAYMAN

RoW 987 Continued...	RoW cars MY 2005-2007 Minor	RoW cars MY 2005-2007 Major	RoW cars MY 2008 On Minor	RoW cars MY 2008 On Major
Additional maintenance for drive belt				
Check drive belt at 36,000 miles (60,000 km) or every 4 years			X	X
Check drive belt at 84,000 miles (140,000 km) or every 10 years			X	X
Check drive belt at 132,000 miles (220,000 km) or every 16 years			X	X
Check drive belt at 40,000 miles (60,000 km) or every 4 years	X	X		
Check drive belt at 100,000 miles (150,000 km) or every 10 years	X	X		
Check drive belt at 160,000 miles (240,000 km) or every 16 years	X	X		
Additional maintenance for convertible top				
Maintain and care for convertible top at 12,000 miles (20,000 km) or every 2 years			X	X
Maintain and care for convertible top at 20,000 miles (30,000 km) or every 2 years	X	X		
Additional maintenance 60,000 miles (90,000 km) or every 6 years				
Replace drive belt	X	X	X	X
PDK Change clutch oil				
Additional maintenance every 108,000 miles (180,000 km) or 12 years				
Change manual transmission oil			X	X
Change Tiptronic transmission oil and ATF filter			X	X
Change Tiptronic transmission final drive oil			X	X
Additional maintenance every 120,000 miles (180,000 km) or 12 years				
Change manual transmission oil	X	X		
Change Tiptronic transmission oil and ATF filter	X	X		
Change Tiptronic transmission final drive oil	X	X		
Change PDK transmission oil				

PORSCHE BOXSTER & CAYMAN

RoW 987 *Continued...*	RoW cars MY 2005-2007		RoW cars MY 2008 0n	
	Minor	Major	Minor	Major
Every 2 years				
Change brake fluid	X	X	X	X
File Condition Report for Long-Life guarantee	X	X	X	X
Every 4 years				
Replace tire sealant	X	X	X	X
After 4, then every 2 years				
Check battery for the tire pressure monitoring system	X	X	X	X
After 4, 8, 10, then every 2 years				
Inspect airbag system	X	X	X	X
Assembly and running gear mounts: Visual inspection of all rubber/hydraulic mounts for damage	X	X	X	X
Road Test Check				
Remote control, front seats, foot brake and parking brake (also operating travel), engine, clutch, steering, transmission, ParkAssist, automatic speed control, PSM switch, PASM switch, Sport switch, heater, air-conditioning system and instruments: Check operation	X	X	X	X
Oils, fluids: Visual inspection for leaks	X	X	X	X
NOTES				
Note: If the mileage for scheduled minor maintenance is not reached, Minor maintenance must be performed no later than after 2, 6, 10..... years.	X			
Note: If the mileage for scheduled minor/intermediate maintenance is not reached, Minor/intermediate maintenance must be performed no later than after 2, 5, 8, 11..... years.			X	
Note: If the mileage for scheduled major maintenance is not reached, Major maintenance must be performed no later than after 3, 6, 9, 12..... years.				X
Note: If the mileage for scheduled major maintenance is not reached, Major maintenance must be performed no later than after 4, 8, 12..... years.		X		

The terms 'check' and 'inspection' include all necessary subsequent work such as adjusting, readjusting, correcting and topping off, but do not include repairing, replacing and reconditioning parts or assemblies.

Ultimate Owners' Guide

ENGINE

Overview

The Boxster and Cayman use a 6-cylinder engine in the classic Porsche 'flat' layout. This means the engine has 2 banks of 3 cylinders in a 180 degree horizontally-opposed configuration. A major departure from previous Porsche flat-6 engines is the adoption of water cooling, both for thermal efficiency (water cooling has superior heat dissipation to air cooling) and noise legislation reasons.

The horizontal layout allows for very compact dimensions, low weight and a low centre of gravity – all important considerations when used in the mid-engined Boxster range (as well as in the larger 996/997 models).

The engine range was given the overall designation of M96 within Porsche. This same basic design has been used (with progressive improvements over the years) to the latest version used in the Generation 2 cars launched in 2009. In these latest models, the engine has been significantly redesigned and has gained the new type number 9A1.

92 Ultimate Owners' Guide

Engine layout

The first model to use the new M96 engine was the original Boxster in 1996. This had a 85.5mm bore and 72mm stroke to give a displacement of 2,480cc. The compression ratio was 11.0:1 and maximum power was 204bhp (150kW). Maximum torque was an impressive 245Nm (181lbft).

As Porsche had done with the 928 engine many years before - when it first introduced Nikasil cylinder bores cast directly in to the crankcase - the M96 engine pioneered another new manufacturing technique. The aluminium crankcase halves are cast around highly porous silicon cylinder liners. The aluminium flows into the porous liners during the casting process, filling the voids in the liners and creating a bore surface that is extremely hard wearing, holds oil well and can be final machined without any further treatment. These integrated liners are known as Locasil liners.

The pistons used in these bores are also aluminium, but iron coated (as they were on the 928/944/968). The crankshaft has seven main bearings and 12 counterweights to reduce vibrations. There are 2 camshafts per cylinder head, which use Variocam technology to modify the inlet valve timing, ensuring the optimal torque curve throughout the rev range.

To keep the engine as short as possible, and as the cylinder banks are offset in relation to each other, the left camshafts are driven from the front of the cylinder block, and the right camshafts from the back. In order to do this Porsche take a chain drive off the crankshaft to a hollow intermediate shaft, which runs below the crankshaft from front to rear of the engine, the camshafts are driven via chains and gears from this intermediate shaft.

The lubrication system is what Porsche term an 'integrated dry sump' method,

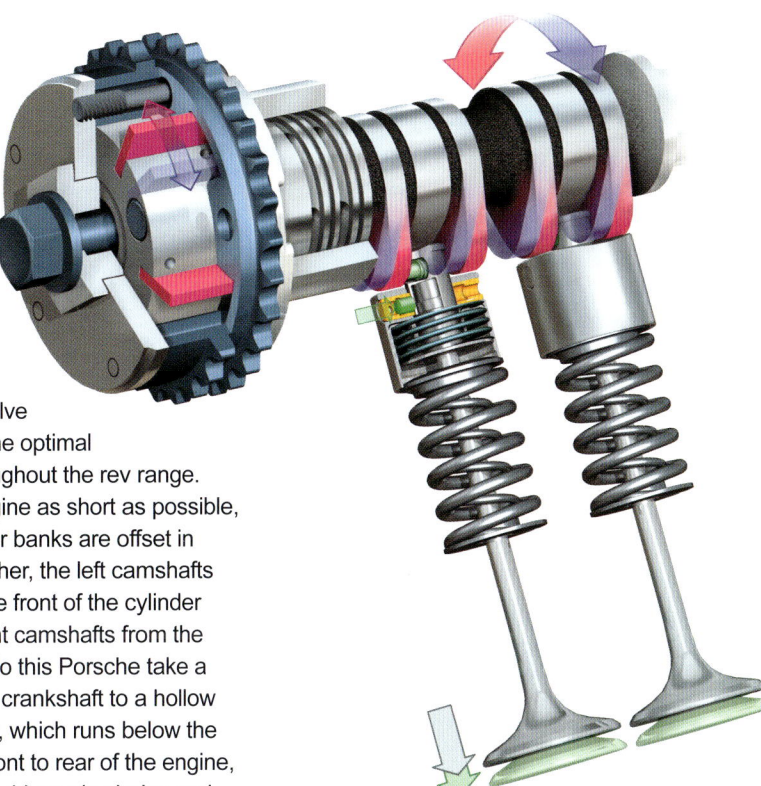

The later VarioCam Plus valve drive arrangement can adjust both valve timing and lift

Ultimate Owners' Guide   93

PORSCHE BOXSTER & CAYMAN

The camshafts are driven by an intermediate shaft, itself driven from the crankshaft

which means that the oil is contained within the engine itself, rather than the separate container used by previous flat-6 models. This reduces the number of scavenge pumps required as most of the oil returns by gravity and only the cylinder heads need separate scavenge pumps. The oil pump is also driven from the intermediate shaft.

Over the years Porsche has increased the capacity of the engine in several steps from 2.5-litres to 2.7- and 2.9-litres for the base Boxster and from 3.2- to 3.4-litres for the Boxster S. The Variocam was improved in 2003 to Variocam Plus, which provided variable inlet valve lift as well as variable timing of the opening/closing. The design of various components was also improved, including the progressive strengthening of the intermediate shaft and its driving gear.

The Cayman S of 2005 used a 3.4 litre variant of the M96/05 engine used in the 997, with a reduced crankshaft stroke giving the smaller capacity (the 997 having 3.6 litres). This engine is designated the M97/21 and has revised cylinder heads and Variocam-Plus. This engine was also used later in the 3.4-litre first generation 987 Boxster S.

The 2009 Generation 2 Boxster and Cayman models may not have received much of an external cosmetic change, but they had a far bigger change under their skins. The engine was heavily revised with the M-series engine series ceasing and being replaced by the new 9A1 engine. The new engine is simplified and has fewer parts. However performance is, as usual, much improved over its predecessor with better power output, improved fuel consumption and lower emissions levels.

The block halves have been completely redesigned and the intermediate shaft has been eliminated. The drive chain for the camshafts is now taken directly from the crankshaft.

Problems
Rear Main Seal (RMS)
It would be impossible to write a book about owning a Boxster (or indeed any

A leak at the crankcase/gearbox seam is an indication of a worn oil seal

of the new generation Porsche models from 1996) without discussion of the now-infamous RMS issue.

Although it doesn't affect every car and is actually only a small oil leak, the problem has seemingly taken on a reputation on a far more catastrophic scale. So what is an RMS and what is the problem?

There is an oil seal at the rear of the engine (at the gearbox end) that seals the crankshaft within the two halves of the crankcase. The crankshaft itself is held within a bearing cage rather than being directly mounted in the crankcase in the way most engines are designed. Various specialists have commented that this sometimes appears to allow the seal to shift slightly after running for a while. This can result in a small amount of oil seeping past the seal. This usually just results in a little oil residue showing under the crankcase (often referred to as 'sweating'), with perhaps a coin-sized spot of oil under the car once a month, Many experts would advise that an engine oil leak on this small scale could be ignored until the clutch is replaced (assuming the car is a manual gearbox version!). Access to the RMS (and the similar intermediate shaft oil seal) is easy when the clutch is removed.

On rare occasions sufficient oil can leak though to form a visible dripping, or actually require topping up. In this case there is nothing else to do other than have a new RMS fitted. Unfortunately this is a job that takes about 6 hours, due mostly to the need to remove the gearbox from the rear of the car, to allow access to the seal.

Those with a Porsche warranty will find that this is now covered and Porsche will replace the seal even when it is just sweating a little. This may well have contributed to the high maintenance reputation this has built up amongst some owners. In fact in many cases, a sweating RMS could be left alone and the owner would likely never notice – especially if the car is not garaged – making any spots of oil go unnoticed.

Make no mistake – if the seal does leak visibly then it must be replaced. Oil that has leaked on to the road and motorcycles (for instance) do not mix. However if

The much-discussed rear main seal has acquired a poor reputation on the M96 engine

there is no visible leak, and you have no warranty, then it can usually wait until the next time the clutch needs changing.

What have Porsche themselves done about the issue? On the quality of the design itself and the scale of the problem, they remain understandably quiet. Nevertheless, there have been revisions to the design of both the seal itself and to the tool used to push it in to place in the crankcase. If the seal needs to be replaced then the latest versions of both the seal and the seating tool should be used regardless of how old the Boxster is. There is no value in using the older versions. The latest version at the time of writing is part number 997.101.21.00 and has a green assembly sleeve. However it is recommended to always check with your Porsche dealer as newer versions may become available.

The Porsche special tool is part number 9609/1

These seal and tool revisions have progressively improved the situation and leaks have reduced in frequency.

Just to complicate things the RMS has been found not to be the sole cause of leaks. Both the intermediate shaft flange bolts (3 off) and the bolts holding the crankcase halves together in the area of the flywheel (4 bolts) have been found to be the source of leaks – and these were often blamed erroneously on the RMS! Porsche now advise that these bolts should now be replaced with new versions that have a sealant coating on the threads and heads.

The latest Boxster (released in early 2009) now has the previously mentioned type 9A1 engine with a redesigned block, and this would appear to have virtually eliminated the problem.

Intermediate Shaft failure

Far more disastrous is failure of the Intermediate shaft. All versions of the M96 engine have experienced occasional failure – although as previously mentioned the design has been revised in an attempt to engineer out the weak points. Sadly the revisions do not appear to have completely eliminated failure, although they have much improved matters.

Porsche have never released details of exactly how the intermediate shaft failures occur. Indeed getting an acknowledgement that a failure is not a one-off ("never heard of it happening before" or "complete surprise" are the often heard comments from Porsche service managers!) is extremely rare. Unfortunately failure of the Intermediate Shaft is almost certain to result in catastrophic failure of other components in the valve-train, due to the fact that the camshafts are driven via chains from the intermediate shaft.

Cylinder failures

There can be 2 types of cylinder failure, both thankfully rare. In the very early cars there was a small batch of engines that failed due to the Locasil bores not fully curing and becoming porous. There are also reports of 'slipped sleeves'. However these may be another name for the porous failure. References are conflicting

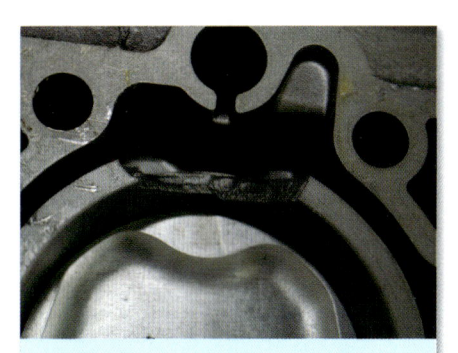

Locasil liner failure on an early M96 engine would usually have catastrophic results

on this issue. Finally there have been incidences of 'D-chunk' failure, where the high silicon content of the bores has actually caused them to be too brittle, and a D-shaped chunk has actually broken off the middle cylinder of the block. This has been most prevalent on the 3.4 litre engine used in the early 996, where the particular combination of using the same block as the 3.2 Boxster engine, but with larger bores, caused the wall of the particular cylinder to be thinner than any other size variant at that point.

Smoke on startup
Occasionally, when you start your car, you may get a cloud of smoke coming out of the exhaust. While this could usually be regarded as an indicator of some sort of problem with the engine in many cars, in a car with a horizontally-opposed engine such as the Boxster or Cayman, as long as the smoke only lasts a few seconds (and then clears), it is usually nothing to worry about. Of course it will invariably happen when you have a crowd of onlookers just for that maximum embarrassment effect!

White Smoke
White smoke is fairly common in cars that are used for short journeys, and then parked for a while. It is normally just condensation - mostly in the exhaust system - burning off. It will usually happen the first time you start the car in the morning, and not happen when the car is already warmed up. If however it happens when the car is up to operating temperature or if the smoke does not clear, it would indicate that there is coolant getting in to the engine somewhere and this will require investigation by Porsche or a specialist. If you are losing coolant then don't just ignore it, get the car fixed and don't use it until it is - running out of coolant can be catastrophic for the engine, and the wallet.

Black Smoke
A burst of black/grey smoke for a couple of seconds on startup is usually just another characteristic of the flat engine layout. Unlike most engines, having the pistons in a horizontal orientation can mean a little oil sometimes seeps past the piston rings and in to the cylinders, while the car is not being used. This oil will then burn off as soon as the car is started. This is something that happens now and again, and is harmless. However a similar caveat to the caution given with the white smoke situation applies. If the car does this regularly, or does not stop smoking after a few seconds, get it investigated. It will need fixing.

Engine DIY tasks
Accessing the Engine
Gaining access to the engine is not as impossible as legend would have you believe. Indeed it will only take a couple of minutes once you have done it once and so found out where everything is!

For a 986 the first thing to do is open the roof a little – leave about a 10cm/4-inch gap between the front of the roof and the windscreen rail. This will open up the 'clamshell' behind the passenger compartment.

Detach the roof lining (if fitted) from the

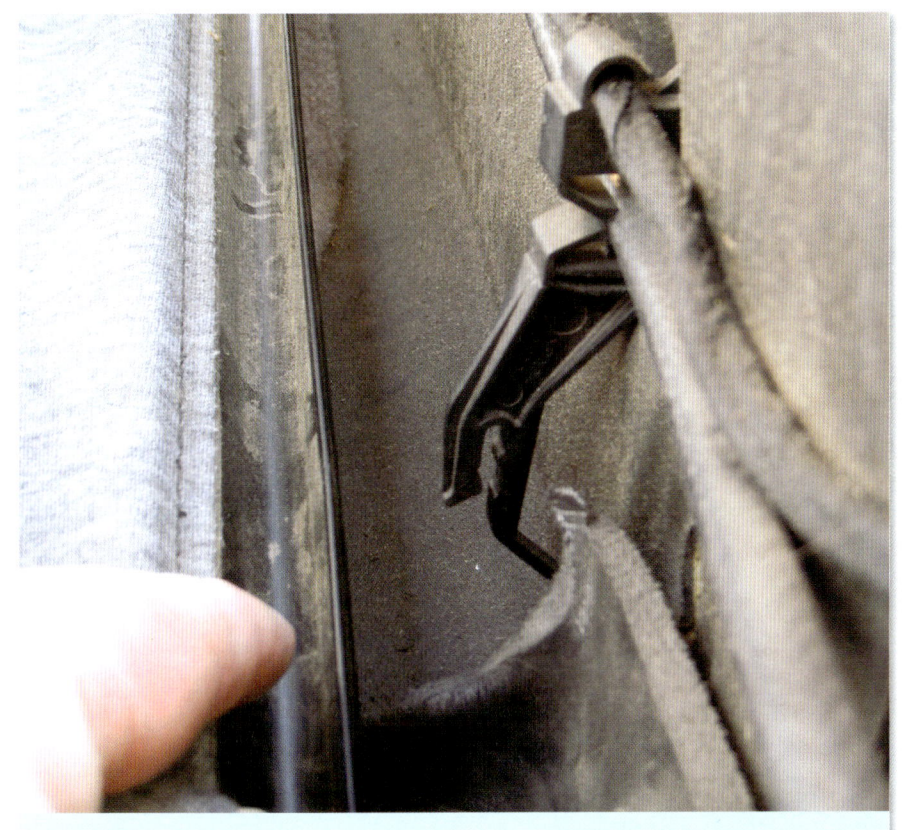

PORSCHE BOXSTER & CAYMAN

clips at the rear of the roof compartment – this is attached with a 'U'-shaped channel – just push down to unclip.

Next unclip the tension cables – there is one each side. These are held at the bottom by ball-shaped press-on clips. Just pull outwards on the ball and it will unclip.

You can now lift up the lower-rear edge of the roof and fold it up and forward, you will feel it engage in to position. Be careful when folding to make sure the plastic window (if you have one) is folded

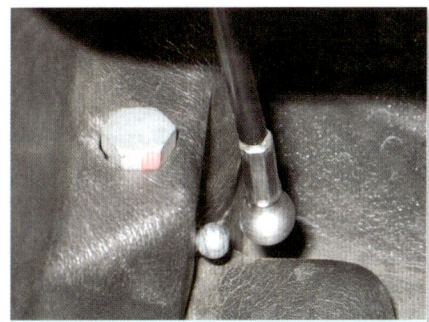

Detach the roof lining from the clips at the rear of the roof compartment

Carefully pull off cup-shaped clips on the tension cables at each side of the roof

Ultimate Owners' Guide   **99**

PORSCHE BOXSTER & CAYMAN

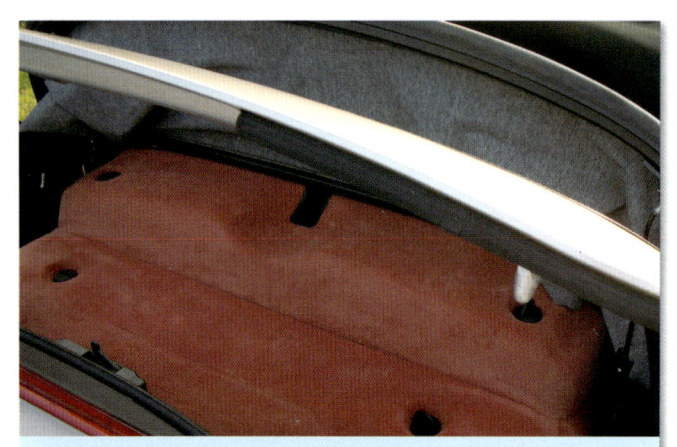

Hinge the roof forward to reveal the carpet and storage box half turn fasteners (4, with 2 at each side)

Lift out the storage box first, then remove the carpet

smoothly – as you would when lowering the roof.

Next either unhook the luggage net, remove the storage bag or the storage box (depending on which your car has) from above the engine compartment. The luggage net is held by hooks attached to the roll-over bar. The storage box is held by half-turn turn-locks on the top. If you have the Digital Sound Processing audio option, don't forget to disconnect the plug connecting the loudspeakers.

Remove the carpet covering the top of the engine compartment – this is held on by 2 more turn-locks. (If you have the luggage net, there are 2 more turn-locks at the front to be removed).

The engine compartment lid itself is removed by turning all 5 of the wire turn fasteners through 90 degrees to disengage and lifting the lid off.

The 987 is similar, but the roof needs to be opened wider – about 60cm (2ft), and the balls at the end of the tension cables are at the top instead of the bottom.

When you fold the rear of the roof forwards, push down on the top of the glass window, then take the tension strap that is supplied Velcroed under the rear of the roof, and bring it forward, around and

100 Ultimate Owners' Guide

Release the 5 wire half-turn clips to remove the engine cover

under the top to clip to the top guide.

The remainder of the procedure is the same as for the 986.

To replace it all, unusually, reassembly really is the reverse of removal!

Removing the top cover of the engine is not the only access to the engine. There is another panel behind the seats that is used to access the polyrib ancillary drive belt – see that section on replacing the polyrib belt for instructions on how to gain access to this area.

Topping up coolant (and maintaining right mixture without airlocks)

If you are losing coolant then the source of the leak should be investigated. See the section on the expansion tank for a common cause. Other causes can be holed or corroded radiators, or of course an old and failing hose. Whatever the cause it is critical not to let the engine overheat. Warped cylinder heads are not going to be a cheap fix…

Having said that, it might be necessary to top up the coolant at some point or other during your ownership of the car. Always use Porsche coolant additive – it is designed to last the life of the car and helps reduce internal aluminium corrosion. Other store-bought antifreeze may not mix well with the Porsche product. I have heard of the coolant being turned to a gel when an owner used a different brand coolant to top up the car. This required it all to be flushed out at a Porsche Centre…

In an emergency, clear water can be used, but refilling to a 50-50 Porsche-water mix should be done as soon as possible after any problem causing the loss is fixed.

The long run from radiators at the front to engine in the middle of the car can mean air locks can occur if you just top up at the coolant filler, if this happens follow this process:

In the rear compartment remove the

coolant cap and the oil filler cap (make sure the engine is cold first to prevent possible injury from boiling coolant).

Lever up the trim cover underneath the filler necks.

Flip up the coolant bleeder valve locking clip.

Replace the oil filler cap

For automatic transmission cars, remove the fuse B1 in the fusebox – this disables the shut off valve for the ATF cooler.

The coolant bleeder valve locking clip is in front of the coolant and oil filler necks

Fill with the 50-50 Porsche coolant additive-water mix. Fill to the MAX line in the level indicator.

Run the engine at idle, continue to top off the coolant until no more can be added.

Do not allow the coolant to exceed 80 degrees C (176F).

Replace the coolant cap and tighten. Let the engine warm for 10 or so minutes at 2500rpm. When the engine is fully warmed up the radiator cooling fans will come on. Run a further 5 minutes at 2500rpm, and blip the throttle now and again to 5000 rpm.

Cover the coolant reservoir cap with a thick cloth and open slowly, releasing the pressure very carefully – do not scald yourself!

Top up the coolant, close the cap again, and repeat the process for a further 5 minutes, revving intermittently to 5000 rpm.

Idle the engine until the radiator fans have cycled on and off once, then switch off the engine and again carefully remove the reservoir cap, taking care to relieve the pressure slowly.

Top up the coolant until it is at the MAX mark on the level indicator in the rear boot.

Flip the coolant bleeder valve locking clip down again.

Replace the filler neck trim cover and all caps.

Replace fuse B1 on automatic transmission cars.

Replace coolant cap
A short note to say that Porsche redesigned the coolant filler cap early in the life of the car. If the part number ends with "00" then a new one should be obtained from Porsche to replace it.

Expansion tank
If you get a flashing temperature light then a common cause is a cracked expansion tank. Apart from a loss of coolant, an easy way to tell if the tank is the cause is to pull up the carpet in the rear luggage compartment, if the tank is leaking then you will see coolant under the carpet. If the area is dry then the loss is likely to be elsewhere, top up the coolant and check

PORSCHE BOXSTER & CAYMAN

under the car for the source of the leak. Don't forget the radiators are at the front of the car and the coolant pipes run the length of the car to the engine.

If the expansion tank is the cause, the fix is reasonably cheap, being the cost of a new tank plus coolant. However as it can be fiddly to do, you might want to get your Porsche specialist to carry out the work.

Oil and filter change

If you do a lot of track days, or if you just feel it adds security, you might wish the change the oil and filter more regularly than specified in the service schedule. Thankfully changing the oil and filter on the Boxster is refreshingly easy.

You will need 8.75 litres of oil (or 8.5 if you are not changing the filter). Mobil 1 is the Porsche recommendation and this is what is fitted at the factory. The weight of the oil is usually SAE 0W-40. Although any oil that meets the specification in the handbook can be used. I personally would use the fully-synthetic options as they will be more stable over temperature range extremes and mileage.

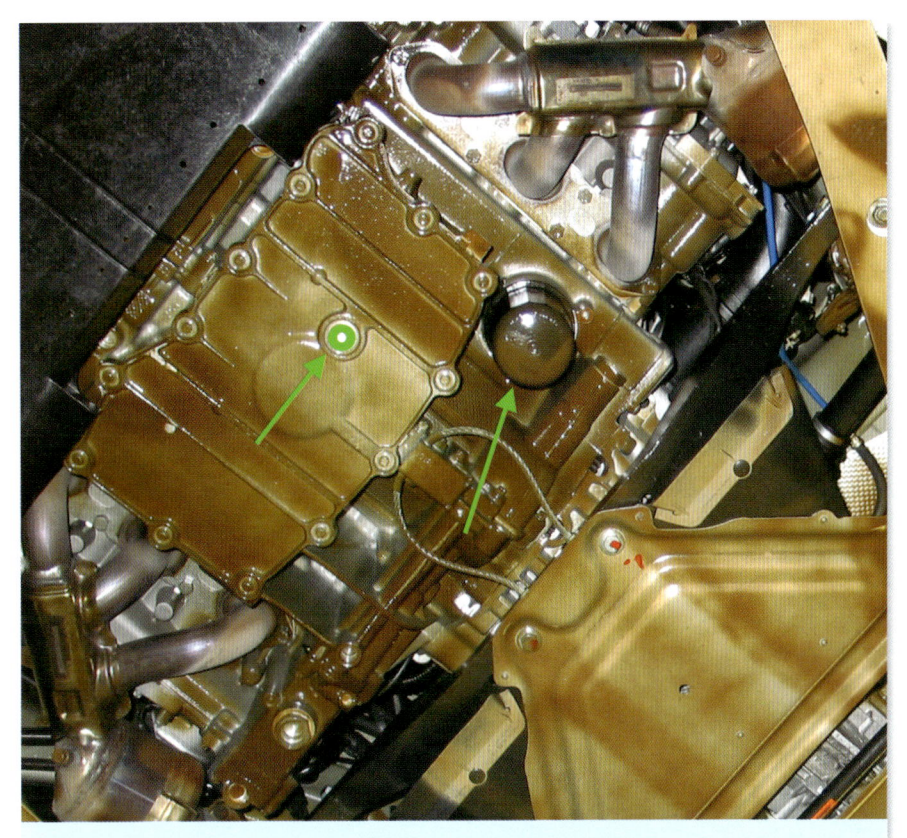

The oil filter and drain plug located underneath the engine

Ultimate Owners' Guide

PORSCHE BOXSTER & CAYMAN

You will also need a new Porsche oil filter insert, which comes complete with a new rubber sealing ring, an 8mm allen wrench, and an oil filter wrench – preferably one that is 74mm (2.9") across the flats – although a strap wrench can also be used. Porsche also recommend you use a new sealing washer each time you remove the drain plug so you probably ought to get one when you buy the filter.

The oil filter is held in a plastic housing (rather than being an all-in-one metal canister) so the filter wrench will be needed to avoid damaging the housing.

The engine oil should be warm when you drain it, so run the engine until it is at the normal working temperature.

You will need to jack the car up on the left side to get to the filter (as always take care to support the car securely whilst you are working underneath it).

Place a large oil drain catch container under the drain plug, a good idea I have seen is to place this drain container itself on top of an oil drip tray to catch any spills.

Remove the drain plug using the 8mm Allen wrench – be careful not to burn yourself on the hot engine, exhaust, or the oil as it drains!

Leave the oil to drain for at least 20 minutes, which is a good opportunity to change the filter.

Use the filter wrench or strap to undo the filter housing, the housing will come away – often leaving the old filter still attached to the engine. Remove the old filter and discard (with due thought for the environment!). Push the new filter in to place over the filter base (either way around – there is no top or bottom). Replace the rubber o-ring on the filter housing and oil it lightly. Refit the filter housing by hand, you can feel when the o-ring begins to seat, and the filter housing itself. The correct torque for the filter housing is 25Nm (19lbft) which will only be measurable if you are using the filter wrench. This is not much so don't over-tighten if using a strap!

When the oil has drained re-fit the drain plug, using a new crush washer. The torque for this is 48Nm (35lbft).

Lower the car and fill with 8.75 litres (about 9.5 quarts) of oil, or if you have not replaced the filter 8.5 litres (9 quarts). Remember the oil filler is the one with the yellow cap!

Although the filler has a small built-in funnel a larger one will be helpful here, Porsche design the car to be filled by plumbed-in lines at the dealership, not from oil cans and I'm sure you do not want to get oil on your rear boot carpet. Do not overfill as it is possible to damage seals with an over-pressurised engine – it can be just as damaging as running with too little oil.

Check the oil level with the dipstick (if your model has one) and verify it again using the electronic check on the instruments. Start the car and check for leaks.

Fitting new polyrib drive-belt
The polyrib belt does not drive the camshafts as it would in some cars, but it does drive the following components: coolant pump, alternator, power steering pump, air-conditioning compressor. The belt must be replaced every 48,000 miles.

PORSCHE BOXSTER & CAYMAN

Access to the polyrib drive belt is through the hidden access panel behind the seats

Access to it is through the engine access panel, behind the seats in the passenger compartment.

To change the polyrib belt, first access the top of the engine as described earlier. Next remove the carpeted firewall cover behind the seats by unscrewing the 4 threaded bolts at the top of the carpet. This reveals a removable metal cover

Remove the 7 cover bolts and lift off the panel.

Before you remove the old belt note the

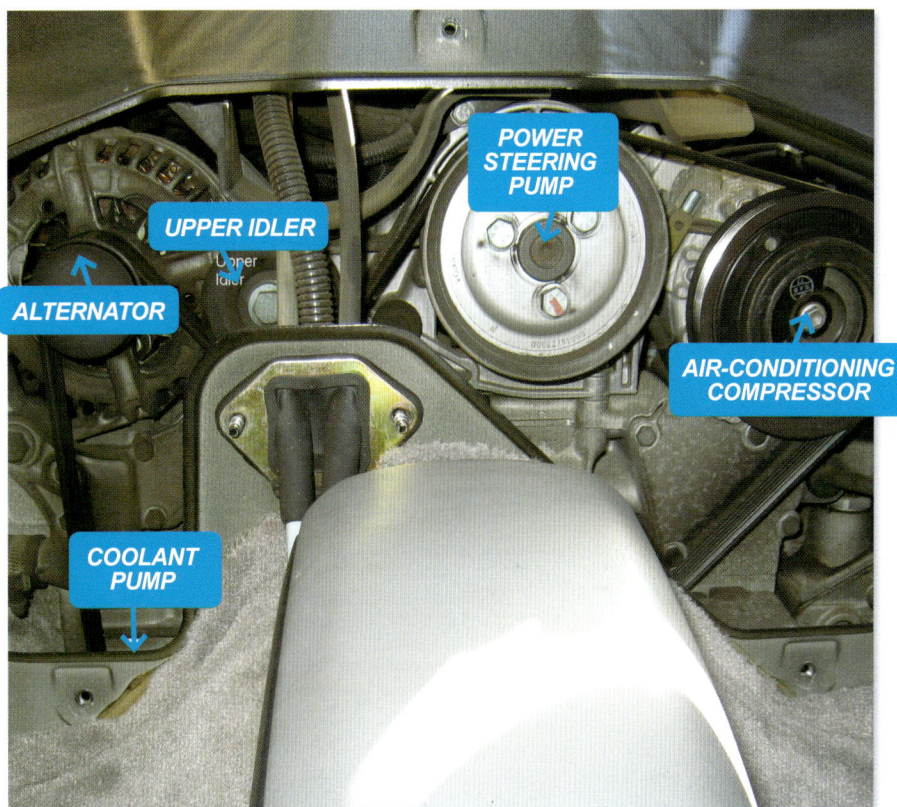

ALTERNATOR — **UPPER IDLER** — **POWER STEERING PUMP** — **AIR-CONDITIONING COMPRESSOR** — **COOLANT PUMP**

The main items driven by the polyrib drive belt

Ultimate Owners' Guide   **105**

PORSCHE BOXSTER & CAYMAN

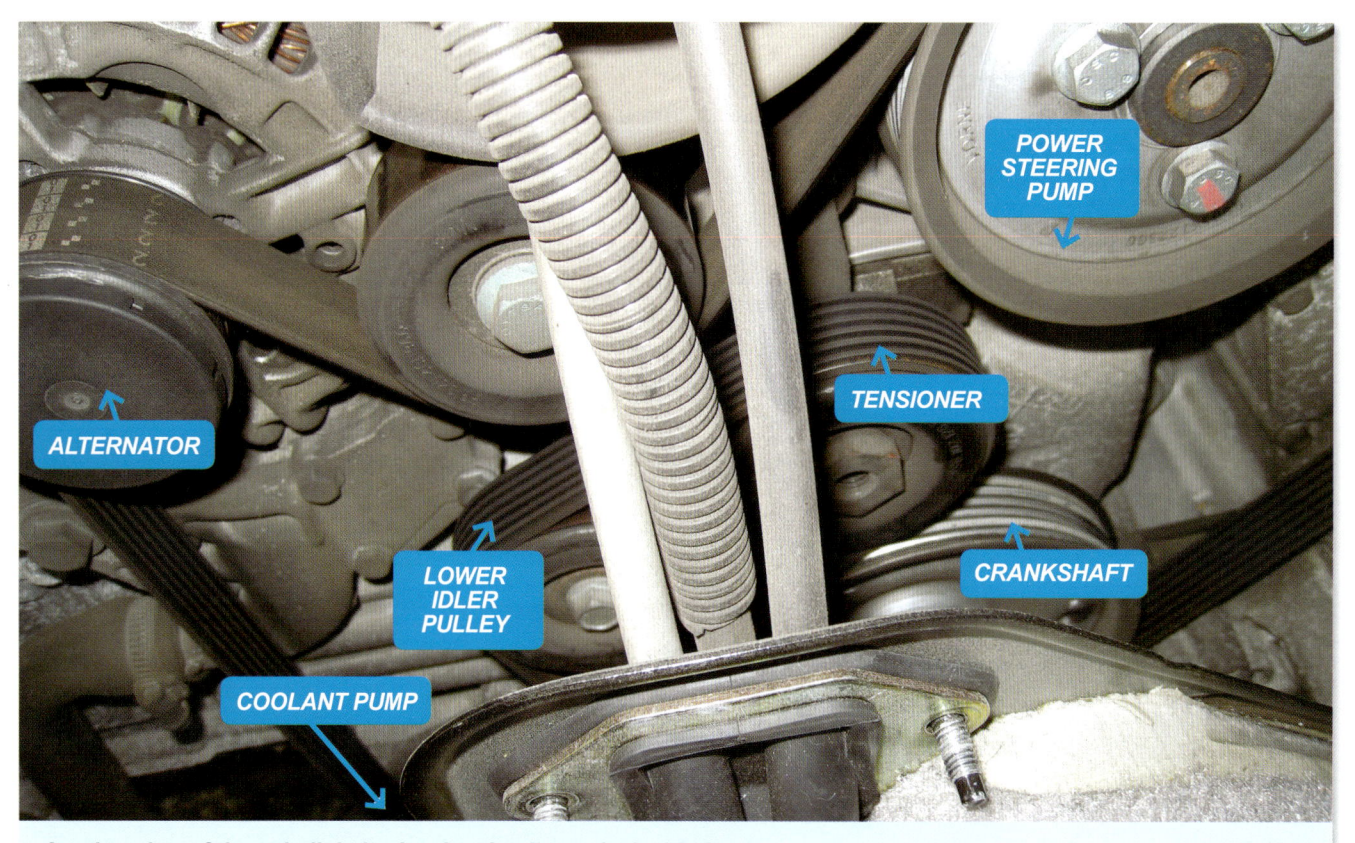

Another view of the polyrib belt, showing the ribs on its inside face

106 Ultimate Owners' Guide

path it takes - you might want to take your own pictures with a digital camera to help with this.

To remove the old belt use a 24mm spanner on the belt tensioner, turn it clockwise to relieve the tension and at the same time slip the belt off the pulleys.

To install the new belt, place it over the pulleys in the following order: coolant pump, alternator, upper idler, power steering pump, air-conditioning compressor, crankshaft, tensioner.

Then use a 24mm spanner to turn the tensioner clockwise, and as you do this slip the belt over the last pulley: the lower idler pulley.

Release the tensioner carefully and check the belt is fitted correctly on all the pulleys. Run the engine to check the operation is correct. DO NOT attempt to touch anything whilst the engine is running - please be extremely careful!

If everything is correct then switch off and refit the engine front access panel, firewall carpet, and refit the top engine access panel.

MAF sensor

If your engine suddenly sounds 'lumpy' at idle, or hesitates under acceleration, there are some components that you can check. The Mass Airflow Sensor (MAF) is one, the oxygen sensors in the exhausts are others, and then there are the coil packs and spark plugs. There are, of course, other causes as well, but fault finding at this stage becomes a specialist job and is beyond the immediate scope of this book.

All these faults can be accompanied by the 'Check Engine' light being illuminated in the dash display.

The MAF sensor in the early cars was prone to getting fouled and causing faults. This is less common on later cars but can still happen. It can sometimes be cleaned but if something is causing it to be fouled then the cause needs to be found or the same problem will just come back.

To access the MAF you need to access

The MAF sensor can be found on the top of the engine's left rear side

the top of the engine (see earlier in this section for the access method). The MAF is located at the rear left corner of the engine compartment, just behind the air filter housing. To remove it you will need to use a tamper-proof Torx bit. Do not touch the wire parts in the sensor with your fingers as this will contaminate them. Use some electronics cleaner to clean it, and once dry reassemble in to its housing (it will only fit in one way).

Exhaust problems and how to fix them

(Cat heat shields, sport exhaust vacuum pipes)

The Boxster has a stainless steel exhaust, which has an extremely long life. There is really only one area that can cause issues – the heatshields above the catalytic converters. These often rattle due to corroded fixings and this can result in a very embarrassing metallic rattle when starting the car. Of course, it will always manifest itself when you have several people near the car – for maximum embarrassment.

Heatshields

The two heatshields over the catalytic converters are held on by 3 sets of fixings each. One or two of these fixings always seem to corrode well before the others – the resultant rattling noise when you start the car should alert you to the need to replace them well before you risk actually losing the relevant heatshield.

The fixings are reachable from underneath the rear of the car. Feel around the top of each catalytic converter box - you can touch the heatshield and check whether it is loose.

The accompanying photo shows a view you can never have – the catalyst heatshields from above – it has been taken 'through' a see-through Boxster that was made by the marketing department of Porsche. This viewpoint shows you the fixing positions in a way that is impossible to show on a real car.

The new fixings themselves are as shown below. They consist of a Dzus-type (quarter-turn) fastener, a thick washer and retaining clip. They are available from your Porsche Parts Counter for a nominal amount.

The old fixings will be easy to remove and you will find there is no

> **SAFETY:**
> ⚠ Never work on the exhaust when the engine has been run for any length of time. Severe burns can result from touching any part of the exhaust system when it is hot.
>
> If you lift the car to work underneath, make sure the car is on level ground, that there are chocks in front of the unlifted wheels and that it is supported by the correct weight axle stands on the appropriate bodyshell hardpoints. Under no circumstances use the car's jack to support the weight of the car.

PORSCHE BOXSTER & CAYMAN

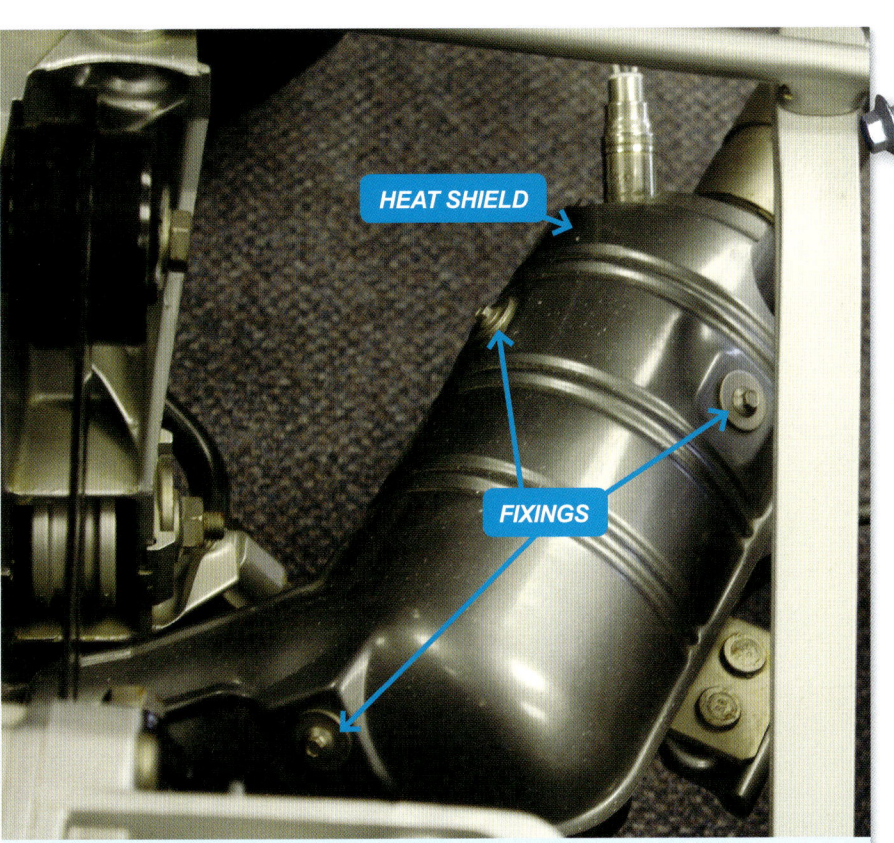

A catalytic converter heat shield as seen from above (HEAT SHIELD, FIXINGS)

Replacement parts for the heat shield fixings are available from a dealer

point in trying to re-use any of the 3 parts that make up each fixing set – they will be too corroded.

To get access to install the new fixings you will probably find that using the socket of a ¼-inch drive socket set – with its associated ratchet handle – gives you just enough room to work above the heatshields, but boy is it fiddly!

Ultimate Owners' Guide **109**

PORSCHE BOXSTER & CAYMAN

The photo shows what you can see from underneath… Note you cannot actually see the fastener from here!

For some reason I always seem to find that I end up not knowing which way I am turning the fixing to get it to latch – it is clockwise of course, but when you are lying under the car and you are trying to attach the fixings without being able to see them, and your hands and arms are getting cramp, all logic seems to go and you wonder if you are turning the right way after all…

Then suddenly everything clicks in to place and the fastener has locked in!

Exhaust Tips
On 2003MY-onwards cars, the exhaust tip can be swapped for an alternative if the owner wishes. That's right, there is no difference whatsoever between the exhausts apart from the tip… So that aggressive-looking twin exhaust on the 'S' is actually just a bolt-on accessory. It's rather disappointing to discover, but a cheap way of upgrading the look of your car if you don't have one.

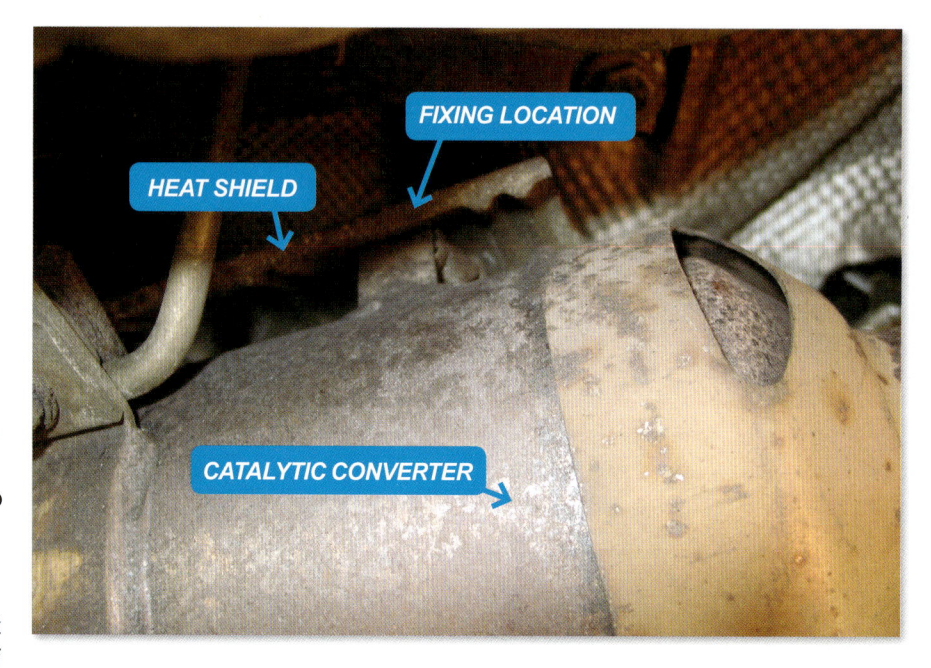

To replace the exhaust tip, just undo the one bolt holding it in place from underneath, and unhook the top from the flange on the silencer box.

This does have the advantage of being able to smarten up a discoloured or corroded exhaust tip – giving the car an instant makeover.

The cars built before this are less easy to smarten up however, as they do have the tips permanently attached. So any change means the whole silencer box has to be replaced.

TRANSMISSION

Overview

The Boxster and Cayman have used various configurations of gearbox over the life of the range. The first Boxsters from 1996 were offered with a choice of 5-speed manual or 5-speed automatic (called Tiptronic S by Porsche) gearboxes. Unusually the gearboxes are cable operated, which Porsche claim has the benefit that vibrations are not transmitted from the engine/gearbox to the gearlever.

The gearboxes were new designs and not related to those fitted to earlier Porsche models. The manual is made by Getrag and the automatic by ZF.

Over time 6-speed manual gearboxes have been added – initially as standard on the S and then as an option on the non-S cars. The automatic Tiptronic S has been refined and has been replaced by the new 'Porsche Doppel Kupplungsgetriebe' (which literally means Porsche double clutch transmission), this is usually shortened to simply PDK.

The gearboxes need little attention – see the Maintenance Schedule for the transmission oil change intervals.

Boxsters and Caymans come with manual and automatic options

Manual gearbox

The manual gearbox in the 1996 car had 5 speeds arranged with 5th and reverse opposite each other in the same plane. The gearbox sits behind the engine and overhangs the rear axle.

Revised ratios were used in the 2.7 when this model was introduced in 1999

Ultimate Owners' Guide   111

PORSCHE BOXSTER & CAYMAN

(for the 2000 Model Year). A 6-speed 'box was used in the Boxster S. This was a development of the 5-speed 'box, but the reverse gear was selected by moving the gearlever far to the left, and forward, the forward gears all being in a normal double-H pattern.

For 2005, the 5-speed 'box gained an improved synchromesh mechanism, which allowed a lighter shifting force and a 27% reduced gear lever travel. However, the 6 speed 'box was redesigned entirely to accommodate the higher torque output of the revised engine. The 6-speed 'box also had a 15% shorter gear lever travel.

From 2005, the 6-speed box from the S was also made available as an option on the Boxster – along with PASM (Porsche Active Stability Management) – as a 'Sport Package'.

The Cayman S was also introduced in 2005, and this uses the same gearbox as the Boxster S (rather unsurprisingly) with slightly taller 1st and 2nd ratios.

Automatic gearbox

Launched at the same time as the manual version, the automatic 'Tiptronic' gearbox offered a two-pedal manual shift experience as well as a full automatic shift. But there was a weight penalty – the Tiptronic gearbox weighed about 50Kg (110lbs) more than the manual.

From 2000, Tiptronic equipped Boxsters

The gearbox is located behind the mid-mounted engine – under the rear load area

MANUAL RATIOS BY MODEL									
Model	Year	1st	2nd	3rd	4th	5th	6th	Reverse	Final Drive
Boxster 2.5	1996	3.500	2.118	1.429	1.029	0.789		3.440	3.889:1
Boxster 2.7	1999	3.500	2.118	1.429	1.091	0.838		3.440	3.56:1
Boxster S 3.2	1999	3.82	2.20	1.52	1.22	1.02	0.84	3.55	3.44:1
987 Boxster	2005	3.500	2.118	1.429	1.091	0.838		3.440	3.75:1
987 Boxster 6 Speed	2005	3.667	2.050	1.407	1.133	0.972	0.822	3.33	3.875:1
987 Boxster S	2005	3.667	2.050	1.407	1.133	0.972	0.822	3.33	3.875:1
Cayman S	2005	3.308	1.950	1.407	1.133	0.972	0.822	3.00	3.875:1
987 Gen 2 Boxster	2009	3.310	1.950	1.410	1.130	0.95	0.81	3.00	3.890:1
Cayman Gen 2	2009	3.67	2.05	1.41	1.13	0.97	0.84	3.33	3.88:1
Cayman S Gen 2	2009	3.31	1.95	1.41	1.13	0.95	0.81	3.00	3.89:1

PORSCHE BOXSTER & CAYMAN

gained a manual override feature – and a designation change to Tiptronic S. This allowed the driver to make gearchanges using the switches on the steering wheel – even when in full automatic mode. After 8 seconds the gearbox returns to full automatic mode unless the car is cornering at greater than 0.5g, is on overrun, or if it is on a steep downwards slope (so you can use engine braking in a low gear downhill).

The 2005 987 carried over the existing

TIPTRONIC GEAR RATIOS BY MODEL

Model	Year	1st	2nd	3rd	4th	5th	6th	Reverse	Final Drive
Boxster 2.5	1996	3.67	2.00	1.41	1.00	0.74		4.10	4.205
Boxster 2.7	1999	3.67	2.00	1.41	1.00	0.74		4.10	4.02
Boxster S	1999	3.67	2.00	1.41	1.00	0.74		4.10	3.73
987 Boxster	2005	3.66	2.00	1.41	1.00	0.74		4.10	4.379
987 Boxster S	2005	3.66	2.00	1.41	1.00	0.74		4.10	3.908
Cayman S	2005	3.67	2.00	1.41	1.00	0.74		4.10	4.161

The Tiptronic gearbox offers a 2-pedal manual and full automatic shifting

Tiptronic transmissions in both the Boxster and S variants. Both had minor changes to adapt them to the higher power and torque of the new engines, and a shorter final drive giving better in-gear acceleration. The 2005 Cayman S used the same gearbox as in the equivalent Boxster S, with a slightly shorter final drive and therefore better acceleration.

PDK
The Generation 2 Boxster and Cayman models dropped Tiptronic S as the automatic gearbox choice, instead the new 'Porsche Doppelkupplungsgetriebe' (PDK) gearbox was offered. The PDK gearbox is a 7 speed automatic gearbox with a double-clutch mechanism – effectively 2 gearboxes in one.

PDK gives tremendously fast gear changes, as the two gearbox shafts have the 1st, 3rd, 5th, and 7th gears on one, and the 2nd, 4th, and 6th on the other. The double clutch allows both to run at the same time, with the power only ever going to one or the other. The double clutch is therefore used to switch the power between the 2 shafts only, and the next higher, or next lower ratio is already engaged the whole time. This results in the virtually instantaneous gearchanges.

The first 6 speeds offer sport driving,

Ultimate Owners' Guide

PORSCHE BOXSTER & CAYMAN

with maximum speed being attained in 6th, the 7th ratio has a high ratio to help fuel consumption whilst cruising.

Fitting a short-shift gear lever

A popular modification for manual cars is to fit a short shift gearlever mechanism. These are available from both Porsche and aftermarket companies. The best known is the B&M 'precision short shifter' which fits all 986 manual transmission Boxsters.

The fitting instructions supplied with this kit are very comprehensive, all I can add are a few hints.

■ If you can't get the old gear knob off, check that your particular one doesn't have a small set-screw that you will need to loosen first. The gear knobs do tend to be very hard to remove – some have had to resort to clamping the old shift lever in a vice in order to exert enough force to remove it. Note that the instructions do advise removing the gear knob before you have detached and removed the old gear lever from the car – take great care not to hit yourself in the face when it suddenly flies upwards!

■ DO remember to mark the cable positions with a permanent marker before removing the cable-end attachments.

■ When you have finished test shift where all the gears are before you start the car. **This is critical for your own safety!**

Enjoy the new feeling that this change brings to your car!

Generation 2 models can have PDK

PDK RATIOS BY MODEL

Model	Year	1st	2nd	3rd	4th	5th	6th	7th	Reverse	Final Drive
Boxster 2.9	2010	3.91	2.29	1.65	1.30	1.08	0.88	0.62	3.55	3.72:1
Boxster S 3.4	2010	3.91	2.29	1.65	1.30	1.08	0.88	0.62	3.55	3.62:1
Cayman 2.9	2010	3.91	2.29	1.65	1.30	1.08	0.88	0.62	3.55	3.72:1
Cayman S 3.4	2010	3.91	2.29	1.65	1.30	1.08	0.88	0.62	3.55	3.62:1

SUSPENSION & STEERING

Overview

The Boxster suspension follows the MacPherson strut principle, with coil-over springs around the dampers. The same layout is used front and rear, with the rear suspension effectively turned through 180 degrees. Incidentally, the 996/997 models of the 911 use the same front suspension as the same year Boxster. Only model-specific items such as spring rates, damper characteristics, brakes etc are different – the main mechanical parts are the same. The rear suspension is different, the rear weight bias of the 911 means that a multi-link design is used instead.

There are differences in the USA and the Rest of the World (RoW) car ride heights – these are detailed later but the USA car rides 10mm (0.4 inches) higher at the front than the RoW car.

Sport suspension (M030)

The Boxster has been available with a Sport Suspension option since it was launched in 1996 and this is available on all models. Initially a 30mm (1.18 inches) lower option (similar to the later GT3) was offered but this proved to be very hard on the road and was soon dropped from the option list. The more usual 'sports' suspension (Porsche code M030) was also available and continued to be offered, although the USA and RoW versions differed in their execution.

The sport suspension is 10mm (0.4 inches) lower in the RoW version, but the USA specification cars are the same height whether or not sport suspension is specified. This has led many USA based owners to change the springs to the RoW spec parts, thereby lowering the car at a stroke.

As well as the lower ride height (where available) the sport suspension consists of harder springs, stiffer anti-roll bars (sway bars) and firmer dampers.

From the experience I have from comparing my own RoW Boxster S with sport suspension, I can confirm that on the road the sport suspension gives a ride

Front suspension follows the tried and tested MacPherson strut principle

Rear suspension uses a similar arrangement but turned around. Note coil spring over the damper

Ultimate Owners' Guide

PORSCHE BOXSTER & CAYMAN

Sport suspension may not be so suitable for urban driving life

SUSPENSION TYPES

Front	Wheel Size	USA: Series and Sport	RoW: Series	RoW: Sport
Front axle height (measured from the road surface to the lower edge of the hex-head bolt of the tension-strut screw connection to the body)	16"	149mm	139mm	129mm
	17"	154mm	144mm	134mm
	18"	155mm	145mm	135mm

Rear	Wheel Size	USA: Series and Sport	RoW: Series	RoW: Sport
Rear axle height (measured from the road surface to the lowest surface of the diagonal brace at the control arm securing point)	16"	144mm	144mm	124mm
	17"	148mm	148mm	138mm
	18"	151mm	151mm	141mm

All above dimensions are to a tolerance of ± 10mm.

that has markedly reduced roll in corners, and less dive and squat under braking and acceleration. The car's attitude is far more consistent and flat. The drawback is that it can give a 'jiggly' ride on poor surfaces and city dwellers may find potholed streets too uncomfortable in a car fitted with the sport suspension option – especially with larger wheel sizes where the reduced height of the tyre sidewall means that there is less cushioning effect available from the tyres.

The accompanying table (for the 986 Model) shows the differences between the USA car and RoW cars on both Series (normal) and Sport suspension.

Boxster S

The Boxster S suspension is based heavily on the standard car, but has different spring rates, and thicker anti-roll bars. Where sport suspension is also specified the spring rates are higher still and anti-roll bars are even thicker, meaning the S on Sport suspension is stiffer still than the standard S.

PASM

For the 987, Porsche offered Porsche Active Suspension Management (PASM) to replace the sport suspension option. PASM allowed switching between a 'normal' running mode for day-to-day driving, and a 'sport' mode, which is ideal for track days and well surfaced roads. The modes are selected by a dash-mounted switch. The normal mode actually appears to be softer than the standard (non-PASM) suspended car, but has the advantage that as the speed

PORSCHE BOXSTER & CAYMAN

DIFFERENCE BETWEEN BOXSTER AND BOXSTER S SUSPENSIONS

Standard suspension	Boxster		Boxster S	
	Front	Rear	Front	Rear
Spring rate (N/mm)	24	27	24	30
Tubular anti-roll bar (diam. mm)	23.1	18.5	23.6	19
Roll bar wall thickness (mm)	3.4	2.5	3.5	2.7

Sport Suspension	Boxster		Boxster S	
	Front	Rear	Front	Rear
Spring rate (N/mm)	30	35.5	30	37
Tubular anti-roll bar (dia mm)	23.6	19.6	24	19.6
Roll bar wall thickness (mm)	3.5	2.6	3.8	2.6

PASM buttons (above) and Sport Chrono stopwatch on dash

increases the damping is also increased to match.

The Sport mode is much stiffer in feel to start with, and also increases the damping force with the car's speed. Switching PASM to Sport also causes the Porsche Stability Management (PSM) system (see the chapter on Brakes) to intervene at higher levels.

PASM components are different to the standard suspension as follows:
■ The dampers are controlled by a by-pass valve and have a continuously variable force.
■ An electronic control unit controls the dampers.
■ Accelerometers monitor the body movements.
■ The switch that enables the driver to select the driving mode.

Other inputs are taken from the PSM sensors for lateral acceleration, steering angle, car speed and brake pressure, and engine torque is taken from the

Ultimate Owners' Guide 117

engine management unit.

Each of the four dampers is individually controlled. Under hard acceleration and braking the front or rear dampers can be instantly stiffened to reduce dive and squat. Likewise each side can be stiffened to reduce roll in fast lane-change manoeuvres or cornering.

The Sport Chrono option on the 987 also operates in conjunction with PASM. This is covered in greater detail in the Instruments chapter.

Steering

The Boxster uses a hydraulically-assisted rack-and-pinion steering system. A safety structure is built in to the steering column to prevent it being pushed towards the driver in event of a crash.

The steering column was adjustable for reach only on the 986, but gained reach and height adjustment with the introduction of the 987.

The steering wheel can optionally have Tiptronic (and later PDK) shift buttons

Multi-function steering wheel on a PDK auto transmission car

mounted on it and a 'multi function' wheel is offered on the 987 models, which allows control of the radio, navigation and telephone without the driver taking a hand off the wheel.

The 987 also introduced a variable steering ratio rack, with progressively lower ratio steering towards each steering full lock. This allows less turns of the wheel to go from lock to lock (only 2.6 turns instead of 3).

Suspension alignment

The Boxster requires little maintenance for the suspension components. However, one operation can have a huge impact on the way the car feels and handles. Having the suspension aligned by an experienced professional, using equipment such as that made by Beissbarth or Hunter can make a world of difference to your car. Using an experienced operator, who specialises in performance car suspension alignment, to set up your car will normally get a better result. They will set the suspension precisely to the correct settings, whereas the local tyre fitter may

987 SUSPENSION	Boxster		Boxster S		Boxster S PASM	
	Front	Rear	Front	Rear	Front	Rear
Spring rate (N/mm)	27	30	27	33	33	40
Tubular anti-roll bar (diam. mm)	23.6	19.0	24	19	2.5	19.6
Roll bar wall thickness (mm)	3.4	2.5	3.8	2.6	3.8	2.6

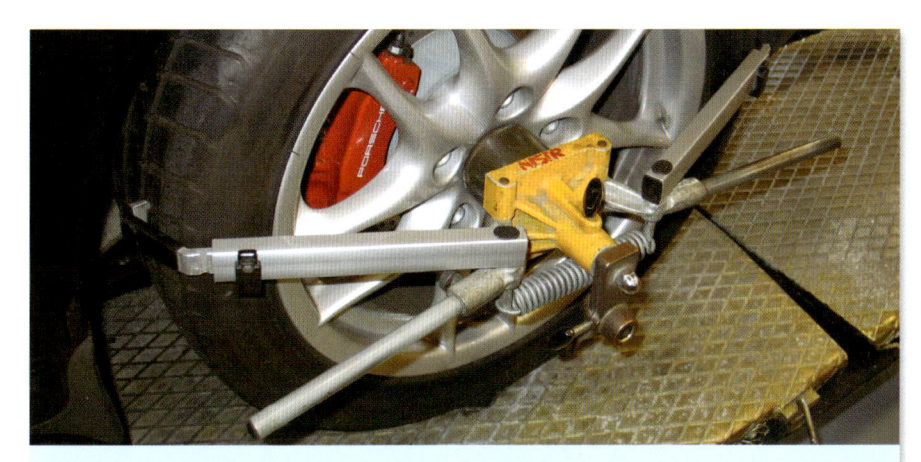

Accurate wheel alignment is a critical part of regular maintenance

just set it to 'within tolerance'. This may cost a little more, but the difference is worth it!

Setting the suspension alignment is something that the home mechanic will not be able to do accurately – not unless they have very deep pockets to spend on something that will be used once or twice a year…

Correct alignment can also save money, preventing premature replacement of the tyres due to incorrect wear and indeed it will also also save wear on other components. I once found I had a vibration above 130mph (I was on an unrestricted autobahn in Germany at the time!) and this was diagnosed by the specialists at well-regarded Porsche specialist and manufacturer Ruf as a wheel imbalance caused by the suspension alignment being slightly out. Evidently it caused a tyre to be scrubbing slightly on one edge, causing that wheel to go out of balance.

Out of balance wheels cause wear on other items as they 'wobble' along – especially dampers and other suspension components. The advice from Ruf was to get the suspension checked at least every year – especially if like me, you have sport suspension.

Typically the suspension is set up after new tyres are fitted, however some operators prefer to have the car in for alignment after it has been on the tyres for a while – the better to see how the tyres are wearing thus indicating any problems. Good operators will be able to set up the car regardless of the tyre condition – the measurements are all done from the wheel rims rather than the tyres.

Note that handling issues may have many other causes even when your suspension alignment is correct. These other factors can include incorrect or non-matching tyres, bent wheel rims, worn or damaged suspension arms and broken or missing deflectors ahead of the front wheels.

PORSCHE BOXSTER & CAYMAN

Knocking noises from the suspension

Sometimes a knocking noise can be heard from the front or back of the car, especially at slow speeds or when it is cold. This is often due to worn 'drop links' (the link arms between the anti-roll (sway) bars and the wheel hubs). These are easy to replace, but changing the rear ones will require a suspension realignment. You can test if the drop links are the cause of the knocking noise by disconnecting one side – the anti-roll bar will now be inoperative and if a short drive on an uneven surface is now silent you will have found the problem.

Another cause of knocking noises from the suspension can be the control arms – replacing these will also need a suspension realignment.

Worn drop link bushes have also been known to cause vibration and vagueness in the steering, so if you have these problems, it may be worth trying new ones as they are quite cheap (assuming your wheels are in balance and all the plastic flaps and scoops are in place – see the chapter covering the Body).

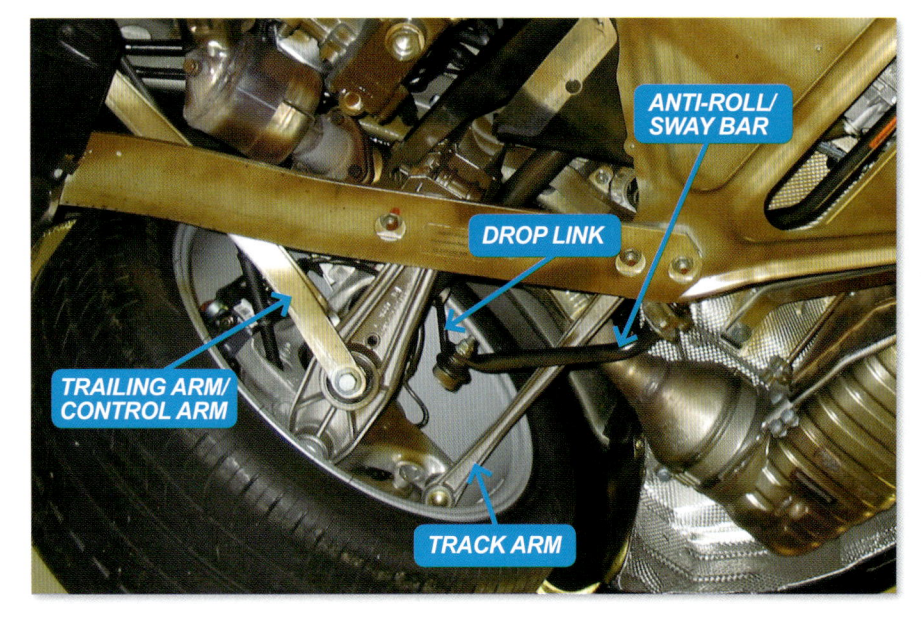

Rear (left) and front (right) suspensions with rear droplink (above)

120 Ultimate Owners' Guide

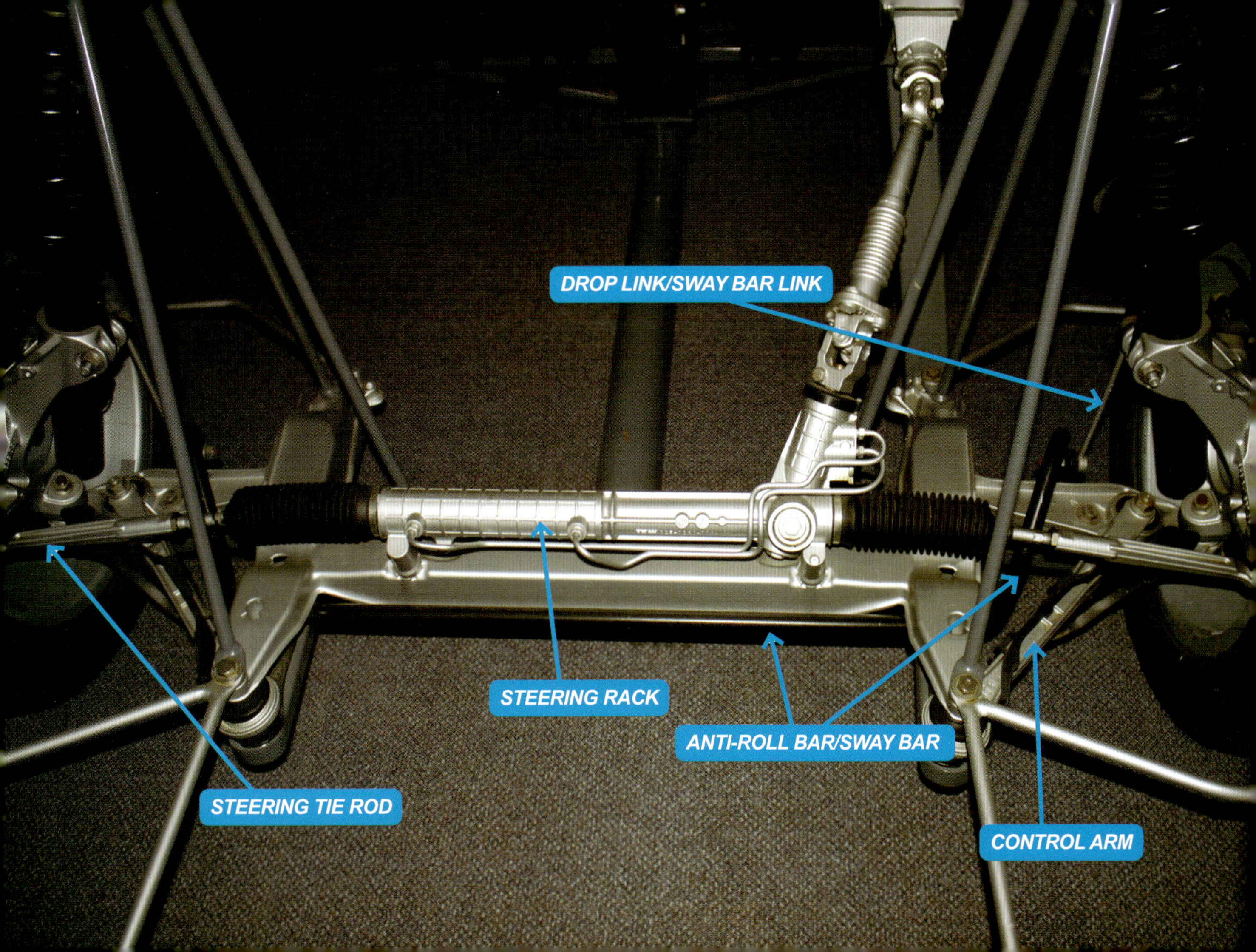
DROP LINK/SWAY BAR LINK
STEERING RACK
ANTI-ROLL BAR/SWAY BAR
STEERING TIE ROD
CONTROL ARM

BRAKES

Overview of the braking system

The brakes on the Boxster have a twin hydraulic circuit operated by a tandem master cylinder, which is operated by a 10-inch vacuum servo. The rear wheel circuit has an integrated pressure relieving valve to help reduce the possibility of rear wheel lock-up under hard braking. All Boxsters have an Anti-lock Braking System (ABS).

The 4-piston calipers are aluminium monobloc units and the Boxster was the first production car to use such units, the concept having been proven for many years on Porsche racing cars. The monobloc design is lighter and stiffer than conventional calipers. The stiffness also contributes to a firm feel to the pedal.

The cast-iron brake discs are internally ventilated, the S additionally has cross-drilled holes in the surface of the discs to improve braking efficiency and clear water away more easily. The S discs are also larger and use the same brakes as the 996. As well as being identifiable by the cross-drillings, the calipers are also painted red on the S. This latter feature immediately differentiates them from the standard models' black painted versions. In 2005, the base model Boxster also gained cross-drilled discs, but retained black calipers to help differentiate it from the more powerful S.

The Parking Brake operates on small brake shoes in an integrated 'drum' brake in the rear disc hubs.

Traction Control was an option on early Boxsters and this worked in conjunction with the ABS and a function called differential slip control (Automatic Brake Differential, ABD) to detect spin of one of the driving wheels. The spinning wheel would then have the brake applied until traction was restored.

PSM

For the 2001 model year Porsche Stability Management (PSM) was offered as an option. Briefly, this takes input from the Traction Control, ABD, engine brake regulation, and sensors for speed, acceleration, deceleration, wheel spin, lateral acceleration sensors and a steering angle sensor. All these inputs are combined and evaluated by the PSM electronics to enhance the stability of the car. Not only can individual wheels be braked by the system, but the engine power can be automatically reduced as well to try and bring a car back that is sensed to be out of control. Nevertheless, it is important to realise that in spite of the Porsche marketing material that demonstrates just how clever and effective the system is, and also despite the beliefs of some owners you might talk to, the ultimate limit is dictated by the 4 small areas of rubber at the bottom of the wheels… In the words of Scotty from Star Trek "I cannae change the laws o' physics". Neither can PSM!

PCCB

Porsche introduced their new Porsche Ceramic Composite Brake (PCCB) system on the Boxster S and Cayman S with the introduction of the 2005 model year. Previously developed on the 911 GT3, the PCCB brakes are 50% lighter than the cast iron brakes, are exceptionally resistant to fade, have a higher coefficient of friction, last 3 to 4 times longer before requiring replacement and do not corrode. The calipers are a similar monoblock design, but have 6 pistons at the front and 4 at the rear. To differentiate the PCCB brakes from the standard versions the calipers are painted yellow.

The PCCB system has been proved to be very efficient, however some owners who do track days are not so keen on them as early versions used on GT3s appeared to have problems with rapid deterioration when used heavily on track – a contradiction to the intended benefits advocated by Porsche. In addition, spinning into a gravel trap could actually cause damage to the disc from the stones that make up the gravel. Later discs have proven much harder wearing, so these concerns should become less relevant. However, great care should still be taken not to accidentally knock the disc – for instance when changing wheels. The discs can break and replacement costs are astronomical.

Rusty discs (rotors)

The Boxster range is known for the fantastic brakes with which they have been fitted and the car has simply incredible stopping power. Despite this, some owners complain (usually just after buying a pre-owned car) that the brakes are terrible! Sometimes it is just that they have stepped out of a car with over-servoed brakes (too much power assistance) and they are just not pressing the brake pedal hard enough.

The Boxster's brakes are very progressive and give good feel – a characteristic often missing from modern hatchbacks and the like, where a brief touch of the brake pedal means having to peel your passenger off the windscreen. However, if you are giving that pedal a reasonable shove and there is not a comforting amount of retardation, this is not because the brakes are inherently poor – it indicates that in this case there is a problem!

Usually it turns out that the previous owner has been in the habit of washing the car and then putting it straight in the garage, often for a few days before it re-emerges once again. After washing, the bodywork has been dried off, but who ever

BRAKE SIZES AND CALIPER COLOURS

Brake Discs	Front	Rear	Caliper Colour
Boxster	298 x 24mm ventilated 4 piston caliper	282 x 20mm ventilated 4 piston caliper	Black
Boxster/ Cayman from 2005MY	298 x 24mm ventilated 4 piston caliper	290 x 20mm ventilated 4 piston caliper	Black
Boxster S/ Cayman S	318 x 28mm ventilated and drilled	298 x 24mm ventilated and drilled	Red
Boxster S/ Cayman S PCCB option	350x34mm ventilated and drilled 6 piston caliper	350x28mm ventilated and drilled 4 piston caliper	Yellow

remembers to dry the brakes?

Unfortunately the normal steel discs (rotors) fitted to modern Porsche cars have a very high iron content (and low chrome content) in comparison with those fitted years ago. This gives them stunning stopping power, but they are more prone to corrosion and incidentally, they tend to wear out rather faster than those in the past.

So what happens if you leave the discs wet after washing? The water is held in both the ventilation cavities and the cross-drill holes and corrosion starts its sinister mission to reduce steel to iron-oxide.

Often, the owner is blissfully unaware of the problem, as the outside faces of the discs tend to clean up quite well after a few applications of the brake pedal. It is on the unseen inner faces – which you can't easily see – that the surface rust doesn't seem to clean off so well and it eats its way into the metal. Because the car is only being retarded by the effort on one side of the disc – the rusty side giving little assistance to stopping, this eventually results in that "My Boxster has terrible brakes" post on a bulletin board somewhere on the internet…

In extreme cases I have actually seen discs with whole chunks missing around the inside face of the disc – and the outer face looks perfectly serviceable!

So what should you do after washing and storing the car?

The easy way to prevent the problem is to take the car for a short drive after washing (as mentioned in the section on car care). This will spin the water out of the ventilation cavities and a few firm applications of the brakes will generate enough heat to evaporate any residual water. This simple action after washing the car can extend the life of the brakes tremendously and save a lot of that hard earned cash!

If you are in the unfortunate position of finding the brakes are already corroded, and a few hard applications of the brakes has not successfully removed the rust, you may be able to get the discs skimmed by a Porsche Service department or a local specialist. However, if the disc thickness is below

If the disc/rotor thickness is not below the minimum, skimming may be an option for rusty brakes

the minimum acceptable, or the corrosion is too entrenched, then replacement is the only action.

Brake pad and disc (rotor) replacement

Replacing the brake pads and discs is a fairly simple job that the home mechanic with the necessary tools and equipment can tackle with confidence.

Be sure though that you do know what you are doing – do not attempt to work on the brakes if you have any doubts

PORSCHE BOXSTER & CAYMAN

whatsoever that you are capable of doing the work correctly or safely. This is your responsibility. You need brakes to **just work** when you need them – this is not a 'fingers crossed' exercise!

The brake discs (or 'rotors' as they are often known) are likely to need replacing when the pads are changed; the life of both items seems to be about the same. Exceptions to this would be if the discs have been skimmed in the past because of uneven wear or surface corrosion, or if you are in the habit of changing pads for a harder compound for track days or driver education track events.

Note that the cross-drilled discs used on the Boxster and Cayman S should not be skimmed.

The table below shows the original disc and pad thickness, and the minimum thickness at which they must be replaced.

Tools required:
- Trolley jack, or a suitable, safe way to lift the car – (not the emergency jack if supplied with the car, this is **only** for wheel changing if you get a puncture while out driving).
- Axle stands
- 10mm Allen key, or preferably 10mm hex bit for socket drive
- Torque wrench
- 19mm socket (for wheel bolts)
- Needle nose pliers
- Screwdriver or small pry bar
- Hammer and nail punch to tap out a retaining pin
- Putty knife or similar flat blade if you have a Boxster S - the old pads have vibration dampers stuck to them
- Philips head screwdriver (an impact driver may be necessary)

Parts Required
- 2 front discs (note the Boxster S has different left and right discs at the front)
- 2 rear discs
- 1 set front pads
- 1 set rear pads
- Anti-rattle clips
- Brake pad wear indicator wires (if worn/activated)
- Aluminium anti-seize compound (Optimoly TA or similar)
- A new retaining pin kit (according to Porsche's recommendations), consisting of a new retaining pin, spring clip, and cotter-pin

If you need to bleed the brakes as well you will also need:
- bleeder tubing
- brake fluid recycling container
- bleeder screw spanner/wrench

BRAKE WEAR SPECIFICATIONS		Pad Thickness New	Pad Thickness Minimum (wear limit)	Pad Thickness Minimum with wear indicator	Brake disc thickness New	Brake disc wear limit
Boxster	Front	11.0mm	2mm	2.5mm	24mm	22mm
	Rear	11.0mm	2mm	2.5mm	20mm	18mm
Boxster S	Front	12.0mm	2mm	2.5mm	28mm	26mm
	Rear	10.5mm	2mm	2.5mm	24mm	22mm

Ultimate Owners' Guide

PORSCHE BOXSTER & CAYMAN

Replacing the brake pads

Make sure you are on a **flat solid surface** – it is not safe to attempt to jack the car up on grass, gravel or soil, even if it is a nice soft surface for you to lie on! Similarly, any kind of sloping ground is not a safe base for lifting a car.

You can jack the whole side up by using the rear jacking point, but ensure you also use axle stands located in positions that will support the car if the jack should fail. The axle stands should only be placed on the bodyshell's hard points and definitely not on any part of the moving suspension or underbody plasticwork. Also be very careful not to trap any of the hydraulic pipes that run the length of the car. If you are in any doubt, seek expert assistance.

You should wear safety glasses for this job. For personal comfort (to avoid skin contact with brake dust etc.) I would suggest latex gloves.

While the car is still on the ground, loosen the wheel bolts slightly (just a ¼ of a turn) with the 19mm socket. Jack the car up using the jacking point nearest the wheel you are working on, or as noted previously, you can raise the whole side in one go if you are replacing both fronts and rears. Raise the car enough that the tyres are clear of the ground.

Place the axle stands in suitable positions (see the section on working safely on your car), and keep the car supported using the jack as well. Now working on only one wheel at a time – again for safety, remove the wheelbolts and wheel.

Remove the brake pad wear indicator wiring harness from the caliper, and then the wear indicators from the brake pads. You will need the needle nose pliers for this, or even a pair of tweezers if your pliers are not small enough.

Remove the spring clip from the retaining pin using needle nose pliers.

Using the hammer and a nail punch or drift, gently tap out the retaining pin. Note: Under the retaining pin is a sprung clip which will fly off when the pin is clear of it. Be prepared for this and try removing the pin by hand after you have driven it out most of the way. Press down on the

Only work on one caliper/disc assembly at a time

The brake pad wear wiring (red) has to be removed first

PORSCHE BOXSTER & CAYMAN

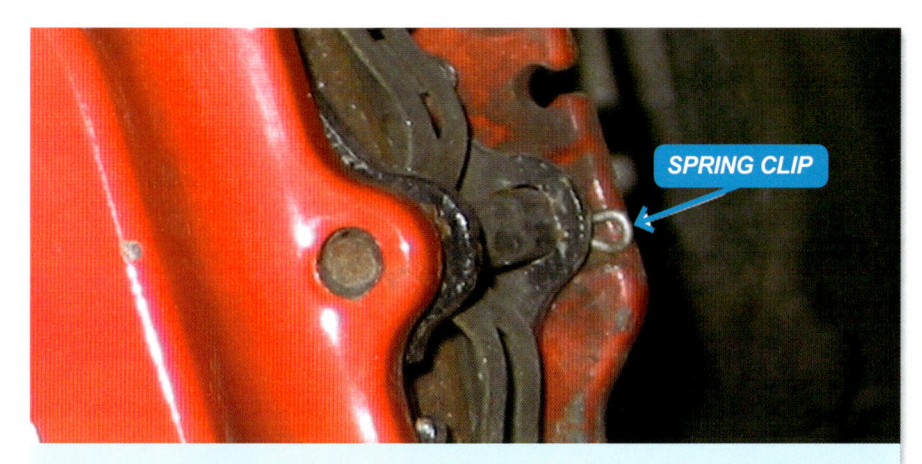

Remove the spring clip (above) first, before tapping out the retaining pin (below)

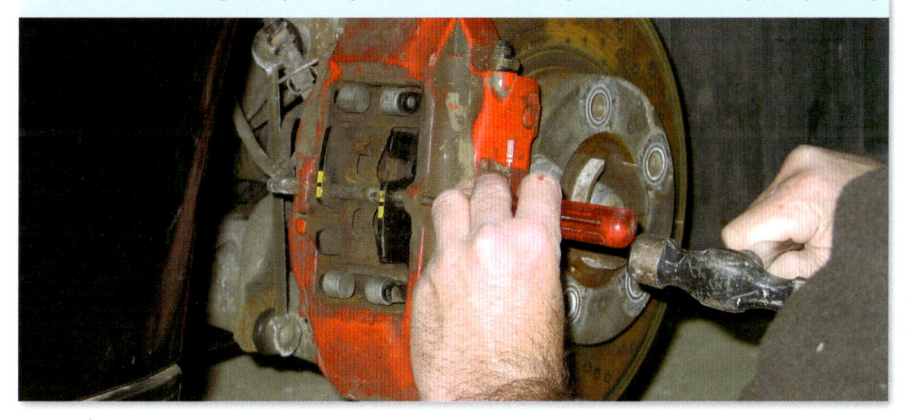

spring clip to take the tension off the pin, and remove the pin with the other hand. When the pin is clear you can remove the sprung clip and slide the pin the rest of the way out without the clip springing out unexpectedly.

Now we need to remove the pads. But before we do so we need to move the pistons back in the calipers to allow room for the new thicker pads. The easiest way to do this is to attach a speed-bleed tube to the bleed nozzle, and open the bleed valve a little using the appropriate spanner or wrench. You can push the pads back in the calipers by carefully using a flat blade screwdriver between the disc and the pad and levering the pads back towards the calipers on each side.

You could also open the brake fluid reservoir and remove some brake fluid first, then push the pads back – but it is far harder to do it this way, and you are pushing the fluid against a lot more resistance. You also need a syringe to remove the fluid from the reservoir to prevent it overflowing. Never just allow the fluid to flow out of either the reservoir or

Ultimate Owners' Guide **127**

PORSCHE BOXSTER & CAYMAN

the bleeder screws – it is a very effective paint stripper and you will damage either the paint on the body, or on the caliper.

Remember to re-tighten the bleed screw after you have pushed the pistons home.

A more professional way to move the pistons is by using the correct pad spreader tool – available from all good car parts shops or motor factors. They are not over expensive and allow the pistons on both sides to be pushed back at once, but the pads will need to be removed first – and in the case of the Boxster S this can be difficult as it uses anti-vibration dampers that help stop the brakes squealing. These anti vibration dampers are glued on to the pad backplate, and have a sprung 'crown' that clips in to the pistons, meaning that you have to cut through the glue using the putty knife or a long flat blade of some kind. It is often easier just to remove the caliper and then extract the pads – which you are likely to have to do anyway as the discs are usually worn.

You will find that the crowns on the damping plates probably get stuck in the pistons anyway (whilst the plate stays stuck to the pad), which means it is easier to remove the caliper to remove the broken part. They are cheap enough so there is no real need to try and salvage the used ones, it is far better to use new ones all around.

If you are replacing the discs (rotors) as well you will want to skip ahead to the *Replacing the discs (rotors)* section, and then return here for the remainder of the pad replacement.

A typical broken damping plate. The damper helps stop squealing

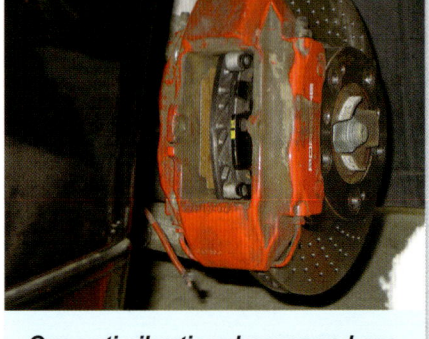

One anti-vibration damper and one pad fitted into the caliper

If you have the Boxster S you will need to clip the anti-vibration damping plate into the piston (with the adhesive backing plate removed), and then slide the pad down into the caliper and into position. You do need to have moved the pistons back into the calipers before you start trying to do this or the pads are not going to go in. Ensure you use the correct damping pad – there are 2 different sizes but they shouldn't fit in the wrong pistons.

Slide the pads in, and then fit a new sprung clip, retaining pin and spring pin.

PORSCHE BOXSTER & CAYMAN

It will be easier to remove the retaining pin in future if a very thin amount of the anti-seize compound is spread on the pin before fitting it (don't get any on the disc or the pads!). You will also need to press down and hold the sprung clip in position whilst you slide the retaining pin in.

Replace the wear indicators and refit the wiring harness for the brake pad wear indicators.

Fit the wheel back on, **hand tighten** the wheel bolts (it is impossible to torque the wheel bolts up with the wheels off the ground) and lower the car to the ground. Torque the wheel bolts to 130Nm (96lbft) once the car is back on the ground.

Press the brake pedal firmly to seat the pads to the operating position. In the S this will also stick the vibration dampers to the pads.

Repeat for the remaining corners of the car, one at a time.

Finally check the brake fluid level.

Replacing the discs (rotors).
Follow the Replace the Pads section to the point where it refers to this section.

Remove the Brake Line bracket retaining bolt. This bracket holds the section of metal brake line between the

Press down and hold the sprung clip as you slide the retaining pin into position

First stage of disc removal is to remove the brake line retaining bolt (arrowed)

Ultimate Owners' Guide   **129**

caliper and the flexible brake line to the suspension strut. The brake line will need to move with it when the caliper is removed.

Note, if you are just replacing the discs, you do not necessarily need to replace the pads, but do so if they are grooved.

Different disc types are used for the Boxster and for the Boxster S. The Boxster has vented discs that are not cross-drilled, the S has larger diameter discs that are ventilated and cross-drilled.

DISC BRAKE DIAMETERS	
Brake Discs	Diameter
Boxster Front	298mm (11.74")
Boxster Rear	292mm (11.50")
Boxster S Front Left	318mm (12.53")
Boxster S Front Right	318mm (12.53")
Boxster S Rear	299mm (11.78")

For the rear brakes ensure the parking brake is released – this means you will need something to chock the wheels to prevent the car moving, also leave the car in gear.

The rear brakes have the parking brake mechanism inside the disc hub – in effect it is a small drum brake contained within the disc itself. To remove the rear brake discs the parking brake will need to be released so that the disc can be removed.

Move the brake assembly round until one of the threaded holes for the wheel bolts is uppermost. Retract the parking brake adjuster by moving the star wheel you can see through this wheel bolt hole upwards using a screwdriver.

Back off the parking brake adjuster by moving the star wheel

As there is no parking brake on the front, the front brake discs do not have this extra complication.

Using the 10mm Allen wrench bit, remove the 2 retaining bolts that hold the caliper to the wheel bearing carrier. The caliper is now free to remove from the disc. Move it to one side. DO NOT let the caliper hang from the brake line – this can damage the brake line or hose. If the line gets damaged then you can lose brake fluid – which could be disastrous. If the

130 Ultimate Owners' Guide

brake hose is damaged I have known them to act as a balloon when you press the brake pedal – the fluid pressure makes them swell up instead of being used to press against the brake pistons. Either way any damage is extremely dangerous to you and others.

To avoid stressing the brake line while the caliper is removed from the wheel hub, either place the caliper on a cardboard box or similar that is the right height, or use a length of wire to suspend the caliper from a convenient point on the chassis.

Remove the countersunk retaining screws from the brake disc using the Philips head screwdriver. If necessary use the impact driver to free them up to start with.

The disc (rotor) will probably be stuck to the hub, to release it use a soft face hammer tapping around the disc. The disc can now be removed from the hub.

To help prevent the rotor sticking to the hub in future use a little anti-seize compound on the inside of the new disc bell where it touches the hub – you will be able to see the contact area by looking at the old one you have just removed.

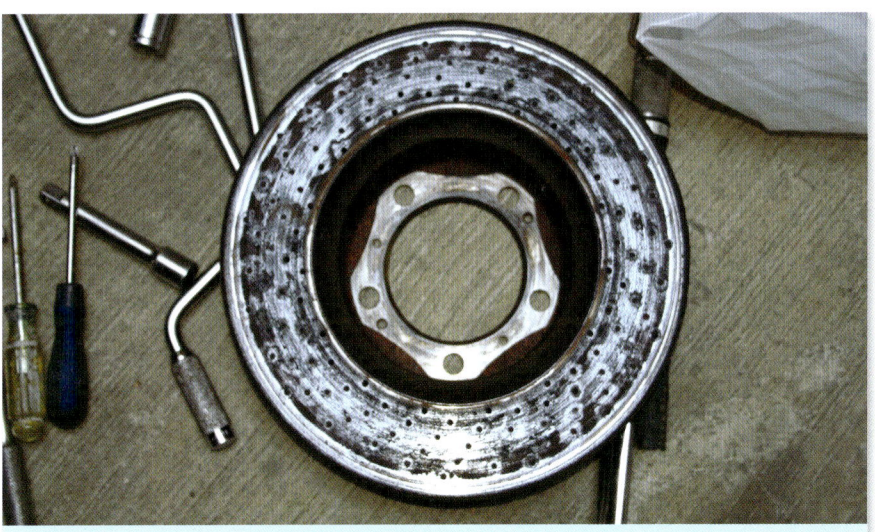

Remove the countersunk Phillips screws from the brake disc hub

Note the clean contact area on the disc hub centre

The new bolts are torqued down to re-attach the caliper

TORQUE SETTINGS	
Brake disc rotor to hub	10 Nm (7.5lbft)
Brake caliper to wheel bearing carrier	85 Nm (63lbft)
Brake line bracket to wheel bearing carrier	10 Nm (7.5lbft)
Wheel bolts	130 Nm (96lbft)

frustration and cost of this.

Reattach the brake line bracket and torque the retaining bolt to 10 Nm (7.5 lbft).

Now you can return to the procedure to replace the brake pads to complete the process.

Ensure the hub itself is clean and now you can fit the new disc.

Line the new disc up on the hub and replace the Philips head screws. These small screws can be given a light wipe with anti-seize compound so they are easy to remove next time. You don't need to do them up too tightly as they are only holding the disc in place while the wheel is not on the car (the wheel clamps the rotor disc against the hub when you torque the wheel bolts up). So just tighten them by hand, and then torque to 10 Nm (7.5lbft) and the next time they won't be difficult to remove!

Now you can reattach the caliper. Use two new 10mm Allen head caliper bolts and once they are fully screwed in, torque them to 85 Nm (63lbft). Some people don't bother using new bolts, but I have known them to seize in when reused, meaning they have to be drilled out and heli-coils fitted to the old threads. It is cheaper to use new ones and avoid the potential

Note - Adjusting the parking brake
On the rear brakes you will need to remember to readjust the parking brake again if you had to back it off.

Open the cover of the rear storage compartment (between the seats) and remove the rubber mat and the bottom panel (you need a T-20 Torx bit to undo the retaining screw). You can now see the handbrake cable adjusting mechanism. Be careful that you do not disturb the car while it is elevated on stands as you are working inside the passenger area.

Loosen the lock and adjusting nuts of the parking brake adjustment.

Back at the rear brake use the small screwdriver to adjust the star click wheel in the upper wheel bolt hole downwards until the brake rotor cannot be turned, and then back it off by clicking it upwards 9 clicks. Repeat this for both rear wheels. Fit the wheels and leave the car elevated on the stands.

Pull the parking brake up 2 clicks, and turn the adjusting nut of the adjustment mechanism until both wheels turn with some resistance.

Release the parking brake and check the wheels turn freely. Ensure the adjusting mechanism lock nut is re-tightened to the adjuster nut.

IMPORTANT!

Do try the brakes at low speed before taking for a gentle test drive. If anything doesn't feel right now is the time to check it!

The parking brake cable adjustment can be found under the rear storage compartment in the centre console

WHEELS & TYRES

Over the years the Boxster range has been available with a wide variety of wheel and tyre sizes. The original Boxster came with 16-inch wheels, with options for 17-inch wheels to be fitted. Later models have been offered by Porsche with anything from 17-inch to 19-inch wheels available from the factory. The following table shows the standard size for each of the different major versions that have been produced.

In general any Porsche Boxster can have larger (and sometimes smaller) wheels fitted from the range shown in the accompanying table, with three important exceptions:

■ Porsche say that pre-1998 models must not be fitted with 18-inch or larger wheels. The suspension pick-up points were redesigned for the 98MY to allow 18-inch wheels to be fitted. The earlier cars were not strong enough to accommodate the increased stresses and shocks that can be transmitted through the lower profile sidewalls of 18-inch and larger tyres.

■ Boxster S models cannot be fitted

WHEEL AND TYRE SIZES	Front		Rear	
Year and Model	Wheel	Tyre	Wheel	Tyre
1996 986	6 J x 16	205/55 ZR 16	7 J x 16	225/50 ZR 16
1999 986S	7 J x 17	205/50 ZR 17	8.5 J x 17	255/40 ZR 17
2003 986	6 J x 16	205/55 ZR 16	7 J x 16	225/50 ZR 16
2003 986S	7 J x 17	205/50 ZR 17	8.5 J x 17	255/40 ZR 17
2005 987	6.5 J x 17	205/55 ZR 17	8 J x 17	235/50 ZR 17
2005 987S	8 J x 18	235/40 ZR 17	9 J x 18	265/40 ZR 18
2009 987 Gen 2	7 J x 17	205/55 ZR 17	8.5 J x 17	235/50 ZR 17
2009 987S Gen 2	8 J x 18	235/40 ZR 18	9 J x 18	265/40 ZR 18
2005 Cayman S	8 J x 18	235/40 ZR 18	9 J x 18	265/40 ZR 18
2006 Cayman	7 J x 17	205/55 ZR 17	8.5 J x 17	235/50 ZR 17
2009 Cayman Gen 2	7 J x 17	205/55 ZR 17	8.5 J x 17	235/50 ZR 17
2009 Cayman S Gen 2	8 J x 18	235/40 ZR 18	9 J x 18	265/40 ZR 18

with wheels smaller than 17-inch as there is not enough clearance between the larger brake disc and calipers and the rims.

- If PCCB brake discs are fitted, these are larger than the standard discs and wheels smaller than supplied by Porsche cannot be fitted.

Checking all items for wear and damage

Tyres should be checked regularly for the correct pressures, visual damage and anything embedded in the tread that could cause a puncture. Check the pressures using a good tyre pressure gauge – don't rely on the one on your local service station forecourt. These can easily have been damaged by previous users, thrown to the ground or driven over.

Buying a good pressure gauge from a reputable parts store, or a motorsport supplier, is a wise investment (I have a Longacre branded one I bought in the UK from Demon Tweeks – www.demon-tweeks.co.uk). Keep it in the car to allow you to check the pressures any time.

Incidentally, I generally prefer analogue to digital gauges, the digital ones tend to only measure to the nearest lb, whereas you can easily see if the pressure is just under or just over with the analogue dial gauges.

The tyre pressures on all 986 and 987 models are:
29psi (2.0bar) front 36psi (2.5bar rear) rear
All pressures are measured cold.
Tyres will get hot when you drive and the pressures increase.
As well as checking the tread for sharp objects, inspect the tyre sidewall for any cuts or bulges – especially if you have caught a kerb.

Tyre age and life

It may come as a surprise to many owners, but tyre manufacturers say that tyres have a finite lifespan. Over time tyres lose their natural oils and they start to crack (perish), which means they are deteriorating and losing grip. This also increases the risk of tyre failure. It is a good policy to replace the tyres after 6 to 10 years. Porsche say 6 years is the maximum. Incidentally, tyres that have been in storage age faster. If they are 6 years old before use then they should not be placed in to service. The effects of ageing are lessened to a degree with tyres that have been in use, but such tyres should be replaced after 10 years as a policy.

The date of manufacture can be easily determined as since 2000 the week and year of manufacture are required to be shown on the sidewall of the tyre. European supplied tyres simply have the 4 number date code: e.g. 1207 would indicate week 12 of 2007. USA supplied tyres have the code as the last 4 digits of a DOT marking – e.g. DOT U2LL LMLR 1207 again shows that the tyre is made in week 12 of 2007. Tyres made before 2000 had a 3 digit code – the assumption being that no tyre would be in service for more than 10 years…

Don't forget the emergency wheel (if you have one). These tend to sit unused, hidden under the cover and forgotten. You might have new tyres

Ultimate Owners' Guide   **135**

PORSCHE BOXSTER & CAYMAN

The manufacture date is shown as a 4 digit number on the sidewall

US tyres have the 4 digit manufacture date identifier at the end of the DOT marking

The EU legal limit for tread depth is 1.6mm, but Porsche suggest 3mm. This is a Michelin Pilot Sport

every couple of years on the rest of the car but the emergency wheel is usually as old as the car.

Tread depth

The legal tread depth minimum allowed in your country or state must (of course) be adhered to. Slicks are great on a dry race track, but slicks cannot expel water. Powerful cars and tyres with no tread on a wet road are a recipe for disaster – or at least a very large repair bill.

In the European Union, the minimum legal tread depth is 1.6mm (about 1/16 inch). Porsche recommend a 3mm minimum, and if it's winter and it rains where you are, this is probably a good compromise between safety margin and cost. Most standard tyres have 8mm of tread when new, and 3mm depth means that usually about twice the legal minimum remains, and 2/3rds of the usable depth has been used.

Repairs

If you get a puncture it is obviously annoying, it is never convenient and can actually mean your car might be out of action for a while. Experience over the last couple of years has shown that periodically, certain sizes and makes of tyre can be out of stock at tyre suppliers – sometimes for extended periods of time. This may mean you have to consider a repair.

Porsche say that the tyres fitted to its

136 Ultimate Owners' Guide

sports cars cannot be repaired. This is not totally true, as subject to the normal constraints of tyre repair (size of puncture, closeness of puncture to the sidewalls etc) they can be repaired. However if you are thinking of running your car down the autobahn at maximum speed day after day (as some of our German friends do indeed do) then Porsche may have a point – I wouldn't want to be relying on a damaged tyre at 160mph. This is where you have to make your own value judgement. Is your style of driving suitable with a (possibly badly) repaired tyre?

New tyres

Whether you have tyres repaired or not, at some point you will need new tyres. There are a few things to remember when you have them fitted. New tyres will have traces of release agent from the manufacturing process still on them and it can sometimes take five hundred miles (800km) of normal driving before this wears off and full grip is attained. When tyres are fitted, the workshop will use a lubricant on the tyre bead to help them fit the tyre over the rim. This can actually allow the tyre to rotate on the rim until this has been washed and worn away. This means the tyres will go out of balance, so avoid any burn outs or traffic light drag-races immediately after fitting! If replacing tyres, you should replace both tyres on an axle at the same time. This is especially important if PSM is fitted as different tyre sizes on the same axle can fool the control unit into thinking that the car is in a constant state of spin! Porsche advise that the maximum difference in tread depth to avoid such problems is 30%.

What tyres to use? You should use the same specification tyres all around the car – unless it is a system tyre such as the Pirelli PZero Asimmetrico and Direzionale

Tyre tread pattern on a Continetal Sport Contact 2 tyre

PORSCHE BOXSTER & CAYMAN

System, which has different tyres patterns front and rear that are designed to work together as a system.

N-Ratings

Porsche works together with major tyre companies to develop tyres that are specifically tailored to their cars. Caution must be used to ensure that the ones you are buying are actually these specific tyres. The manufacturers often have tyres of the same name and size in their ranges, but the Porsche tyres often have different construction and even tread patterns to the standard ones. For this reason all Porsche-specific tyres have a 'N' designation which is followed by a number (N0, N1, N2 etc).

The way this works is when a tyre manufacturer has a new tyre design, they submit it to Porsche for testing. When the tyre passes the testing (which is a collaborative effort from both the tyre manufacturer and Porsche) the tyre is given the designation 'N0'. Subsequent developments of that design are again tested and approved, and each one is

Continental (above) and Michelin (below) tyres with Porsche approved N-rating

given the next 'N' number (so N1, N2 etc). When the tyre design is revised completely, or changed dramatically enough from the original, the tyre designation starts again at 'N0' and the whole process starts again.

As well as not mixing tyre types or manufacturers, you should not in principle mix the N types front and rear (and never on the same axle). Use of a good tyre supplier should avoid all of these issues, but it is useful to know the information so you can check they know enough to fit your tyres (if they say "N-what?" or try to tell you non-N tyres are the same as the N-rated ones then it's time to look for another supplier!).

Speed ratings
Use of N-rated tyres will mean that you don't have to worry about the correct speed rating. If you have decided to go outside of the Porsche approved tyre ranges, then you will be needing tyres with a 'Y' speed rating, which is 186mph. This is more than the Boxster range is capable of, but legally what the car was homologated on for each country.

Tyre makes
Porsche tyre partner companies at the time of writing include Continental, Bridgestone, Dunlop, Goodyear, Michelin, Pirelli, and Yokohama. What you get on the car when new is sadly no longer able to be specified. Note that not every make is available for every model year or every size. What make is best? That really depends on the individual driver and what they want from the tyre. Makes that are consistently popular with owners at the time of writing are Michelin, Pirelli and Bridgestone.

Porsche publish the results of the tyre tests every year in their magazine Christophorus (enquire at your local Porsche centre) and from time to time on their website. The results of the current and past years can usually be found in the Christophorus archive at www.porsche.com – although the precise location and availability of the information within the site changes from time to time.

Finally, fitting slicks for Trackdays or Drivers Ed events is not a great idea without some modification to the oil supply (a deeper sump pan and modified baffling as a start). Porsche specifically warn against fitting slicks to the Boxster range as the increased cornering forces these tyres allow can cause oil starvation to the engine.

Wheel options and offsets
There are different opinions on the aftermarket wheels that prevail around the world. In the UK, non-Porsche wheels seem to be regarded by most enthusiasts with suspicion and it is rare to find a car on aftermarket rims. However, in the USA aftermarket wheels seem more popular. There are also wheels that look like genuine Porsche wheels – the size and style is the same or very similar, but they are copies. There is a very quick way that these copies can (usually) be spotted – on each side of the tyre valve on Porsche wheels there are numbers cast in. One is the rim width (in inches) and the other is the offset (in mm). The copy wheels never seem to have this information.

PORSCHE BOXSTER & CAYMAN

So what is the offset? The offset is the measurement of the mounting surface of the wheel hub from the true centerline of the wheel. Knowing this value means you can calculate that your replacement wheels will not be too recessed, or too protruding.

If fitting wider wheels, you also have to be aware that going too wide may mean the wheels foul on the wheelarches on the outside, or against suspension components or brakelines on the inside. You need to be certain that this cannot happen with your new wheels and tyres. Be very careful here as the fouling may not be apparent at the front until the steering lock is fully applied. In addition different makes of tyres of the same size can actually be of different sidewall dimensions and one make may fit where another may not!

Additional information on wheels and tyres

If you want to find more detailed information on wheels and tyres, I can highly recommend the tirerack.com

The wheel rim width (here 7 inches) and offset (here 55mm) is shown either side of the tyre valve on Porsche wheels

140 Ultimate Owners' Guide

website. This American-based website has a massive amount of information on tyre performance, fitting and technical aspects. The information is usually equally applicable to those inside and outside of the USA.

Wheel bolts

Hold on, do you mean wheel nuts? Technically, on modern Porsches they are bolts rather than nuts, but popular terminology refers to them as nuts... And that's what they often drive owners when they corrode… (nuts!)

The problem is that they often corrode on the surface which, although not actually harmful, looks bad. One cause for this seems to be the use of aggressive acid wheel cleaners, which appears to accelerate the corrosion process (which also appears to be inevitable). There are two options open to the owner with corroded bolts: replacement or refurbish. Replacement is easy, Porsche will happily sell you a new set. No problems there apart from the cost. Refurbishment is fairly easy as well, and cheap.

Wheel bolts are relatively easy (and cheap) to restore

The materials needed are some fine emery paper, silver aerosol paint, kitchen towel, masking tape, and some aluminium grease.

Simply remove one or two of the wheel bolts from each wheel and clean up just the hexagonal heads using the emery paper. After using the emery paper you can also clean them with some degreaser if you have any available, but for a 'quick and dirty' job it's probably not totally necessary. When you are happy you have the corrosion removed, mask the curved part of the back of the hex head and the thread of the bolt using the tape and kitchen roll and give the heads a light coating of the spay paint. Allow the paint to dry and you can then give them another light coat or two. Let the paint cure thoroughly before fitting back on the car, remembering to lightly grease (with Optimoly TA paste) the bolts threads and in between the bolt head and the spherical cap (do not grease the rounded cap itself). Finally torque the bolts to 130Nm (96lbft). Repeat for the remaining wheel bolts.

If necessary, the locking wheelnut bolts can be refreshed in the same fashion (taking care not to block the security profile).

The end result is certainly worth it as the bolts no longer spoil the look of your nice clean wheels.

Do not be tempted to use a higher tightening torque 'to be safe' as this can result in damage to the wheels or the bolts themselves (or both). In turn, this could result in failure of the damaged item, which, as with anything safety related, is more than undesirable.

As previously mentioned the wheel bolts do have a tendency to show discoloration with surface corrosion. Cleaning these up as described is fine, but some aftermarket companies offer stainless steel replacements. Personally, I would not use stainless steel as it has different characteristics to the normal bolt material. In addition I have seen aftermarket bolts that do not have the correct radius on the mounting surface, meaning that instead of the torque force being applied evenly over the full mounting surface, it is concentrated in a small area. Eventually this can lead to the wheels being damaged and/or coming loose – again not a desirable situation.

If you are tempted to use such aftermarket bolts, try a test fit – you could use a thin layer of engineer's blue, (or maybe permanent marker) on the rounded mating surface. Fit the bolt then remove and see if the engineer's blue has been abraded over the full rounded area – if it hasn't return the bolts to the supplier.

Using the emergency wheel

Guidance for jacking the car and changing wheels can be found in the *Where is everything* chapter. However there are some things to remember when using the emergency wheel.

The wheel is (very obviously) much narrower than the normal wheels on the car. Handling WILL be affected. The wheel has markings on it that says the maximum speed is 50mph (80km/h). It would be foolish in the extreme to ignore this. If you have an accident how culpable will you be if your steering, braking etc is compromised by exceeding the safe capabilities of the emergency wheel?

The emergency wheel is only designed to get you to the nearest tyre depot. It is not designed to be used for days, weeks, or months at a time. Anyone who has had to stick to a lower speed because they have an emergency wheel fitted will know how much of a hazard you suddenly feel on faster roads. You are an unexpectedly slow moving vehicle in among the faster flowing traffic. I had to do it on a Sunday night from Le Mans to the Calais ferry terminal and then home (no tyre centres open on a Sunday night!) – it was a horrible experience I would not wish to repeat!

Of course the spare is only any good as long as you have checked it and made sure it is maintaining the correct pressure. Add this to your routine checks along with the road tyre pressures, oil and water and blocked drain holes!

COOLING, HEATING & VENTILATION

As they are all located together (at least component-wise in the car) the cooling of the engine (radiators) and of the occupants (air conditioning) is covered in this section.

Engine cooling
The engine is water cooled by two radiators mounted at the front of the car. A water pump is integrated in the right-hand cylinder bank. Early Boxsters had 2 radiators, one mounted each side of the nose of the car. The 986 S introduced an additional 3rd radiator in the lower middle of the nose for increased cooling capacity, the additional inlet also adding a slightly more aggressive look to the S. When the 987 superseded the 986, the central radiator was deleted from the S variant, unless it was also a Tiptronic. In this case an oil/water intercooler took over the central location. To maintain the frontal differentiation of an S over a standard car, the central radiator cavity itself was retained, although the manual cars only had a black plastic blanking panel in the recess!

Coolant capacity is 18 litres (19 litres for Tiptronic cars), rising to 22 and 24 litres on 987 models.

Air conditioning
Air conditioning was offered as an option from the start of production and even in a convertible is a very worthwhile option to have. The Boxster was my first car with air-conditioning and I don't know how I managed without it. The funny thing is that it was a standard fitment on the S when I bought it and at the time, I said I wasn't bothered about it – indeed I didn't want it. How wrong I was! On the very hottest days you can put the roof up when it gets to be too much to bear and within seconds the cabin has cooled down to below 20°C.

The early Boxster and 987s have 2 radiators, each ahead of the front wheels

Ultimate Owners' Guide

PORSCHE BOXSTER & CAYMAN

Climate control panel on the 986 Boxster

You'll need to remove the debris regularly!

On track days it is indispensible. Yes, the true race cars do not have it, but I feel the extra freshness and alertness that air-con allows all day long more than outweighs the small extra weight penalty. Professional racing drivers spend all day in the gym ensuring they are fit enough to take the heat. Sadly, my day job precludes me from doing the same!

The condensers for the air conditioning system are located in front of the radiators within the front bumper (they are in effect sandwiched to the radiators).

The heating system uses the same vents into the cabin as the air conditioning. With the Climate Control set to 'Auto', it maintains the cabin temperature by varying both the heating and cooling systems.

Preventative maintenance

The air-conditioning condensers are also located behind the front bumper, in a sandwich with the engine coolant radiators. It is possible to replace the condensers yourself but as the main problem with an under-performing air conditioning system is usually finding where the leaks are, the whole operation is probably best left to a specialist with the necessary testing equipment.

It is worthwhile doing some preventative maintenance now and again. The most important thing to do is to remove the inevitable build-up of leaves, dirt and other rubbish that gets drawn into the radiator inlets. Many service centres don't bother to do this simple task at the annual service. Even if it is checked, the longer service intervals of the 987 models can mean that it is two years between inspections. The debris can react with moisture and road chemicals and can corrode both the condensers and coolant radiators. Leaking condensers are probably the most common reason for a failed air conditioning system (one that doesn't respond to simply regassing the system).

The easiest thing to do is to vacuum out the inlets in the front bumper regularly. You can use a normal household vacuum cleaner to do this – and of course your partner will not mind... (why would they?). However, the grill in the bumper makes it difficult to access the back corner of the recess of the inlets, even normal crevice nozzles are too short, and the back corner is of course where all the debris accumulates. The solution is to get a cardboard tube such as you get in cooking foil (hint: you've already annoyed your partner by using the vacuum to suck up wet leaves. It is possibly best to save the tube from the next empty roll of foil for when you get around to cleaning the radiators – rather than unroll a new roll of foil just for the tube!). Fit the cardboard tube over the vacuum's pipe and flatten the open end enough to slide it through the slats in the bumper to get to the back of the inlets. Simple!

Removing the bumper

For better access, you can remove the bumper and really get to the radiator/heat-exchanger assembly. This is quite simple, but before you start it is better to have a second person available at the point where you actually slide the bumper cover off, and when you begin to refit it.

Details on how to remove the bumper are in the Body chapter.

Re-gassing

Every few years it is necessary to re-gas the air conditioning system. It will become obvious when the air vents no longer pump out cold air when the 'LO' (sic) temperature is selected on the control panel.

You can have this done at many specialists while you wait. Kits are also available which allow you to do the job yourself, although if there are any leaks then you might need to revert to a specialist after all. Note that US Law requires that any person who services a motor vehicle air-conditioner is properly trained and certified. It is advisable to use an anti-bacterial treatment to kill any bacteria in the system that could result in unpleasant odours being emitted from the system while in use.

The service connections are located

PORSCHE BOXSTER & CAYMAN

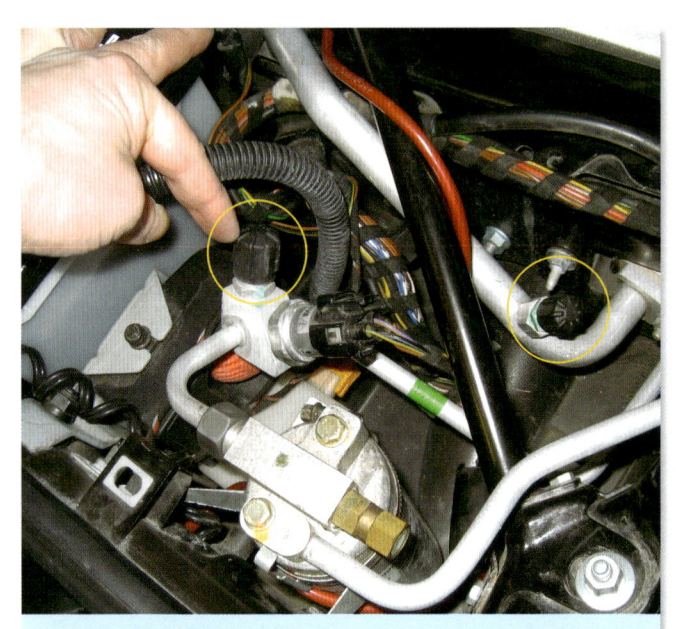

The air conditioning connectors (circled) are found to the left side of the battery

The pollen filter is also to the left of the battery, under a plastic panel beneath the base of the windscreen

in the front compartment, under the plastic panels beside of the battery.

Pollen filter
The last piece of the ventilation system we will cover is the pollen filter. This is accessed by removing the plastic panel to the left side of the battery. The filter is located half under the scuttle at the base of the windscreen. There is an option to have an active charcoal filter for those who suffer from allergies, and the standard pollen filter can be replaced by this active charcoal option if the owner desires. The filter just lifts in and out.

146 Ultimate Owners' Guide

ELECTRICAL SYSTEM

Overview

The electrical system in the Boxster range has evolved over the model years from a traditional point-to-point wiring loom, through to the power-and-controller type of system used on the latest cars.

A 'CAN' bus (Controller Area Network - a wired network) was introduced with the 2001 MY – along with a slightly redesigned instrument cluster. The 2003 MY introduced another development, 'MOST' (Media Oriented Systems Transport), which is a fibre-optic network used for the in-car entertainment systems. Like all mainstream cars today, it uses 12volts DC and has a negative earth.

Battery

The drain on car batteries in modern cars can be considerable. Although both battery and alternator technology has improved over the years we are still reliant on lead-acid 12-volt batteries to start our cars, run lights, air conditioning, sound systems, satellite navigation, tracker devices and if you are Homer Simpson, a microwave oven, deep-fat fryer and waffle maker...

In the old days batteries just had to start the car and power some very dim lights and we had problems with them then! Today we ask so much more from batteries it is a wonder they continue to work so well.

Having said that, Boxster owners have sometimes found that after as little as 2 or 3 weeks of inactivity, the car will not start and the battery is dead, this seems especially to be the case with those fitted with tracker systems or alarm/immobilisers. Experience suggests battery life in a standard Boxster can be as low as 3 years, while some are still going strong after as many as 7 or 8.

So what can be done to mitigate the problem? The best solution to both the problem of keeping a battery fully charged and in the best of health is to use a battery conditioner.

Note: For information on accessing the battery when it is flat, see the section on Emergencies.

Battery Conditioner

A battery conditioner is not a normal car battery charger. Car battery chargers are designed to charge a flat battery quite quickly and must only be used with the battery disconnected from the car, due to the high current involved. Even on the low setting the current used can be high enough to damage a modern car's electronics. A battery conditioner on the other hand is designed to be used on a battery that is already charged, but where the car will not be used for a while. Indeed, battery conditioners are not designed to charge a battery that is flat. It monitors the voltage from the battery and, if it drops by a small amount, charges the battery at a very low amperage – too low to damage the car's electronics. When the battery is fully charged again, it switches the charging current off and continues to monitor the voltage, kicking in again if it drops....and so on.

This means that the battery conditioner can be left connected to the battery continuously while the car is garaged, and it will maintain the battery at the optimum

PORSCHE BOXSTER & CAYMAN

performance for far longer than would be the case if one is not used.

There are two ways battery conditioners normally connect to the battery, either directly onto the battery terminals (by crocodile clips or via a small hard-wired loom and connector), or by plugging into the accessory power socket.

If using the direct-to-the-battery method, you will want to be able to close the front luggage compartment, but at first glance this looks impossible without clamping the conditioner lead in the seal. However there is a way that you can close and secure the car while it is connected, this is by routing the wire either out of the top of the bonnet (hood) by the wipers, or by running it down the length of the bonnet in the channel on the outside of the seal and out by the corner at the top of the front PU bumper.

I have made a slight modification on my car that enables me to plug and unplug the trickle charger without removing the battery cover, I cut a small amount of material away under the finger-recess that is used to lift the cover. This allows the charger lead to be plugged/unplugged easily.

If you are using the type of charger that plugs into the accessory socket, Porsche have provided a cutout in the bottom of the door seal to allow the conditioner lead to feed out. This won't trap the lead if you have to close the door and will avoid having to drop the window a crack to feed the lead out.

There is one more thing to check if you are using the accessory socket. Establish if the socket is live with the ignition off. On some cars Porsche have configured the socket to switch the power off after a couple of hours once the key is removed from the ignition. This is to prevent battery drain if an accessory such as a satellite navigation device or radar detector is left plugged in. If the socket in your car is switched in this way you will need to get it permanently activated at a Porsche service centre or a specialist. Alternatively you can opt for the conditioner type that

The battery conditioner lead routed out past the wipers

The lead can be routed out past the headlight at the front bumper

PORSCHE BOXSTER & CAYMAN

Battery cover modified so conditioner lead can be permanently located

water until the level touches the tab. When topping up, wear safety glasses and be careful not to splash the acid from the cell up into your face or eyes – it WILL burn. You can use a small mirror to observe the levels while you are topping up to prevent any possibility of getting splashed.

Battery replacement

Replacing the battery is fairly straightforward, but there are a few things to remember to save causing yourself problems afterwards and possible deafness during the process!

If you have a pre-2003MY car, and it is fitted with the factory-fit radio/cd/cassette, then you need to have the radio-code available. This is because if you disconnect the battery for more than a few seconds you will need to enter the radio code to re-enable it. If you have the Porsche (Becker) model CR-23 – or the built in systems in the 987 models, then they are coded to the ECU and an activating code is not required.

Most Porsche cars have built-in alarm systems these days, and the sirens have

is connected to the battery and avoid the problem altogether.

Topping up the battery

With the battery being hidden away under that neat plastic cover at the rear of the front compartment, it is easy to forget to check the battery acid level. However, as Porsche use non-sealed batteries it is something that does need to be done every now and then.

To check the level, start by removing the cover. Turn the two plastic fasteners half a turn and pull up the cover from the front. This reveals the battery underneath. Begin by undoing the caps over each battery cell (a medium-sized coin is about the right size for the slots in the caps). Take a look inside each cell and see where the acid level is. If it is difficult to see use a torch, NOT a cigarette lighter or match (as there is a risk of fire)! Within each cell, there is a little indicator tab that can be seen only from directly above. Top up with distilled

Ultimate Owners' Guide

PORSCHE BOXSTER & CAYMAN

their own back up batteries. Disconnecting the main battery will be detected by the alarm system as an attempt to beat the alarm, and of course the siren will sound! This is extremely loud and in a confined area such as a home garage will be most painful. The way to avoid this is to prove you own the car – by having the correct key.... The process is to make sure everything electrical is off, then insert the ignition key and turn it to the position where the ignition is on – but do not start the car.

Leave the key in this position throughout the replacement procedure and the alarm will not be triggered.

The battery is very heavy and great care should be taken when lifting it out of the shelf and away from the car. Work out before you do anything how you can most comfortably and safely remove the battery. If you have any doubts about being able to do this, have a trained mechanic do it for you. You may find it more comfortable and safer to step right into the front luggage area to get the right lifting position. Have an assistant standing by to receive the battery as you lift it out.

Remove the positive terminal first and ensure it cannot touch any metal surface – it is best to ensure this by wrapping electrical tape or similar around the terminal.

Remove the negative (earth) terminal.

Detach the battery vent hose.

Using a 13mm socket and extension, remove the fastener holding the battery clamp in place.

Refitting is the reverse. Make sure that the battery is located correctly on its shelf, refit the clamp and tighten the fastener.

You may find the new battery has the vent adaptor already fitted – at the wrong end. There is a plug in the 'correct' end that you can remove and swap to the other end.

Connect the positive lead first, then the negative. The torque settings are below. It is important not to tighten too much – just enough to secure everything, and not too tight – it is important not to damage the battery casing or the clamp terminals.

Remove the ignition key.

You might find after fitting the new battery that the power windows have lost their memorized position at the top of their travel. To reset this, raise the windows once to the top and then press the "up" side of the window rocker switch again to store the final position.

BATTERY FIXING TORQUES	
Battery clamp	23 Nm (17 lbft)
Battery terminal clamp to battery post	5 Nm (4 lbft)

iPod connection

Be honest, you've just bought yourself a Boxster and the most important question you have right now is "How do I get my iPod working in my Boxster?"

There are many answers and many of them very expensive. But if you have a 986 and the standard radio/CD, there is a cheap way that doesn't involve the inconvenience and poor sound of FM transmitters, and the functionally is far better. I have an iPod Classic with 160Gb of music working in my car.

If you have either the CD changer preparation kit, or a CD player fitted in the front luggage compartment, you are most of the way there. (If not – see later for parts you can buy).

First check you can put the existing radio/CD unit into a mode that accepts input from an accessory (or AUX) input. Basically if you have a button marked 'TP' on the radio then you should be able to enable AUX.

Turn the radio ON, and press and hold the TP button for about 8 seconds until 'Becker 1' or 'Porsche 1' is displayed. Turn the tuning knob until 'AUX OFF' is displayed. Press either button located directly under the arrow symbols on the display to change the present setting from 'OFF' to 'ON'. Turn the radio off. The Auxiliary Audio Input has now been activated.

Now you need to get the signal from the iPod to the AUX input. As indicated earlier, if you have the wires for the CD changer in the front compartment, you just need to connect the iPod to the two phono connectors (the din plug is not needed). Connect the phono plugs of a 3 meter (about 10ft) long, 3.5mm stereo plug to 2 phono plug cable. You will need

3m (10ft) long 3.5mm stereo plug to 2 x phono plug cable

a phono female-to-female stereo adaptor to connect the 2 pairs of phono jacks together (unless you are lucky enough to find a 3 meter long, 3.5mm stereo plug to 2xPhono socket cable).

Now route the cable through to the passenger compartment. I passed it through a rubber plug in the bulkhead between the luggage area and the scuttle where the battery is located.

Route the cable neatly and where it is not going to interfere with the operation

Route the cable neatly through the bulkhead into the pasenger area

of anything (wipers, access to air conditioning connectors etc). I followed the existing loom as much as possible.

There is another large rubber plug behind the battery that gives access to the passenger compartment.

You can cut a small slit in this with a sharp knife and push the cable through and down. There is carpet tacked to the other side of this so there will be a little resistance. However you will find that you can push the cable down and it will appear

Ultimate Owners' Guide **151**

PORSCHE BOXSTER & CAYMAN

Push the cable through the rubber bung behind the battery

In the cabin, route the cable to where you want the iPod

beneath the dash and against the footwell.

Now just route this to where you wish to use the iPod and plug in. Use cable ties to tidy the cable away and to make sure it cannot get in the way, or get trapped in the pedal mechanism.

When you want to use the iPod you use the 'S' (source) button on the radio to select the AUX input, and just use the iPod controls as normal.

If you want to charge the iPod at the same time, a 12volt charging adaptor is available (made by Belkin among others) that plugs into the accessory socket in the dash. It has a dock connector on a flying lead to connect to the iPod and a 3.5mm socket to allow the dock output to be used instead of the headphone socket. The dock connector does give a better quality sound as well as charging the iPod.

Belkin 'Auto Kit for iPod w/ Dock Connector', part # F8V7058 is what to look for (note: there are various additional letters added to the end of the part number to denote colour).

If you use this you may find (as I did) that you get a whistling noise that rises and falls with the engine speed.

I thought initially this was due to a poor quality cable (so I bought the ultra expensive QED cable shown in the photographs!). However the unwanted noise was actually caused by a ground loop – the accessory socket helping to cause this.

The solution was simply to use a 'Ground loop isolator' at the phono connectors. These are available inexpensively from specialist car audio dealers (in the UK for £5-£10), or even online from retailers such as Amazon. Mine did seem to take a few hours of use to "settle-in", but now it performs brilliantly.

If you do not have the CD Changer wires, do not despair. You can obtain a connector from car audio dealers (e.g. discountcarstereo.com) that allows the use of the AUX connector on the back of the radio – although you will need to obtain the radio removal tools in order to plug it in.

The part number you want is BLAU/8-3.5M and it is an 'Auxiliary Audio Adapter for select Blaupunkt/Porsche Radios'.

If you have the CD changer and wish to retain it in use as well as the iPod, then there is also an adaptor available that allows connection of both. This is an 'Audio switcher/Auxiliary input adapter for select Sony radios' part number SON-AUX.

This technique will work for 986 model Boxsters. Unfortunately 987 and Cayman owners have totally different audio head-units fitted which work using the optical MOST system and the above will not work. It is possible however to use either FM transmitters, or, if you want good sound quality, a Dension aftermarket unit (or similar) will need to be installed. Be aware this may invalidate the Porsche warranty.

Porsche caught up with the rest of the world in late 2008 and 2009 MY cars have the option of a 'Universal audio interface' which has iPod, USB, and Aux inputs. This can be retrofitted if the car does not have it originally.

It is worth noting that from about 2006, it is possible to use MP3 CDs – up to 150 tracks per CD can be accommodated, but only the CD slot can play them (they do not work in the autochanger).

Fitting new lamp bulbs

Replacing the bulbs is (mostly!) very easy. It is highly recommended that you carry a spare set of bulbs with you in the car. In some countries this is a legal requirement.

As can be seen in the table on the following page, there are different bulb types depending on whether you have a 986 or 987. The latest cars have replaced the side lights and rear lights with LED variations. If there is any doubt as to which you have, a call to your Porsche Centre will be able to confirm this (have your chassis number to hand)).

Headlights

If you have a 986, all the front-facing lights are contained within the headlight housing assembly. The 987 migrates the fog lights to a separate housing in the radiator intakes – roughly oblong in shape on the 987, and round on the Cayman.

The headlights themselves come in two versions - with and without Litronic (Xenon) bulbs. Litronic bulbs should

PORSCHE BOXSTER & CAYMAN

BULB CHART	986		987	
Bulb	Type	Rating	Type	Rating
Dipped beam	H7	55 W	H7	55 W
Litronic dipped beam	Philips D 2 S	35W	Philips D 2 S	35W
High beam	H7	55 W	H9	65 W
Additional height beam with Bi-Xenon headlight	n/a		H11	55 W
Front fog lights	H7	55 W	H8	35 W
Rear fog light	P 21	4W	P 21	4W
Direction indicator (RoW)	P 21	4W	PY 21	4W
Turn signal (USA)	MSCD 40		PY 21	4W
Reversing light	P 21	4W	P 21	4W
Brake light	P 21	4W	P 21	4W
Tail light	R	5 W	P21	5 W
Side light	W	5 W	W	5 W
Side light (Litronic)	H	6 W	H	6 W
Direction indicator - side (RoW)	W	5 W	W	5 W
Side marker light (USA)	W	5 W	W	3 W
Interior light	W	6 W	W	6 W
Centre brake light	W	3W	W	3W
Number (license) plate	C	5 W	C	5 W
Luggage compartment	K	10 W	K	10 W
Door guard/kerb light	W	5 W	W	5 W

last for many years and are unlikely to need replacing, therefore you would be unlikely to need one in your emergency set of bulbs.

The Litronic bulb works as the low-beam headlamp, and when you select high-beam with the light stalk the Litronic bulb beam is lifted with a motor to help fill in the light field.

The high beam bulb is always a halogen bulb (as is the low beam on non-litronic lights).

To change the bulbs in the light cluster, you need to remove the light housing from the car:

1 Inside the front luggage compartment, undo the plastic nut holding the carpet in place to each inner wing (fender).

2 Pull the carpet away from the inner wings.

3 On the inner wings, there are 3 plastic covers, and one rubber bung in the middle of them – remove the rubber bung. (The plastic covers are for access to the adjustments for height and lateral movement of the headlights – do not adjust these).

4 Insert the socket wrench from the toolkit over the spindle in the hole the rubber bung was covering. Place the wrench so that the swivelling handle is facing horizontally towards the back of the car.

5 Turn the socket wrench down and towards the front of the car – through 180°. There will be a loud 'Bang!' noise, which is rather disconcerting the first time it happens. Don't worry, it is just the headlight unlatching from the retaining mechanism. The headlight will also move forward slightly from its recess in the front wing.

6 The headlight is now unlocked and can be withdrawn CAREFULLY from the wing. Note that for 986 models with Litronics, there is a separate connection on a flying lead that has to be disconnected with the headlight housing partly removed.

7 Turn the socket back so that it faces vertically down.
Replace bulbs as described below. To replace the assembly:

8 Insert the headlight housing assembly on to the guide rails.

9 If you have a 986 with Litronic headlights, connect the electrical plug connection.

10 Slide the assembly back on the rails into the wing. Note: For 986s with

Extra connection lead for Litronic

the Litronic headlights ensure that the wiring loom connected in the step above has not fallen forward at the last second and over the main connector – I have had this happen to me in the past and it resulted in the side light not working. Very frustrating, as it took a long time to work out what the problem was! I now use a thin rule to hold the wire out of the way until the headlight is almost home.

11 Push the headlight firmly home, and at the same time turn the socket wrench until it points horizontally to the rear once more – again you will hear a loud 'Crack' as the locking device engages.

12 Ensure the headlight is fully engaged and locked by trying to pull it forward – it should not move. (You don't want to find that it is not fully fitted the first time you next have to brake hard!)

13 Remove the socket tool and replace it in the toolkit – or if you are like me and have to do this regularly to swap the headlights from the UK's left dip to neutral for driving in Europe (see later) then I keep the tool in the centre armrest cubby.

PORSCHE BOXSTER & CAYMAN

14 Replace the rubber plug and secure the carpet back into place – it fits under the edge of the rubber boot seal.

15 Check that all the lights function correctly.

Headlight Bulbs

The headlight bulbs are accessed from under the cover at the rear of the headlight housing. On the 986 this is just clipped on. On the 987 there are 4 screws to remove as well, (I'm not sure why – I don't recall anyone ever complaining that their cover had come loose on the 986).

Halogen bulbs

The halogen bulbs (whether both dip and main-beam, or just main-beam) are replaced by pulling the connector off the pins, and then unclipping the wire retaining clip. The bulb can now be withdrawn.

When installing the replacement bulb ensure you do not touch the glass with your bare fingers. The bulbs run very hot and the acid from your fingers will burn into the glass – degrading the light quality.

Ensure the bulb is seated correctly –

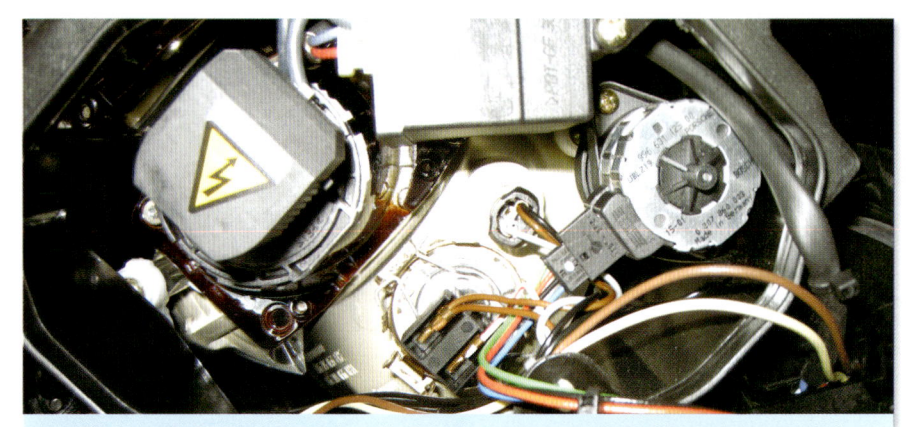

Inside headlight housing (above); Squeeze the retaining clip to remove the halogen bulb (below, left); Rotate retaining collar to remove Litronic (below)

156 Ultimate Owners' Guide

there is only one way around that it will fit properly – and clip the wire retainer on. Finally, push the connector back on to the pins.

Litronic bulbs
The Litronic bulbs are changed by turning the plug that holds the bulb counter-clockwise (it has a bayonet fit) and pulling the plug off the bulb.

On the 986, the bulb is held with a clamping ring. Turn this counter-clockwise and remove.

On the 987 the bulb is retained with a wire retaining clip – this is disengaged at the end with the loops.

Replace the bulb, ensuring you do not touch the glass as before (always a good policy with bulbs anyway).

Reassemble in the reverse order (clamping ring or wire clip). Note that the bulb only fits in in one orientation, the retaining ring also fits in only one orientation.

Replace the plug and turn clockwise to the stop.

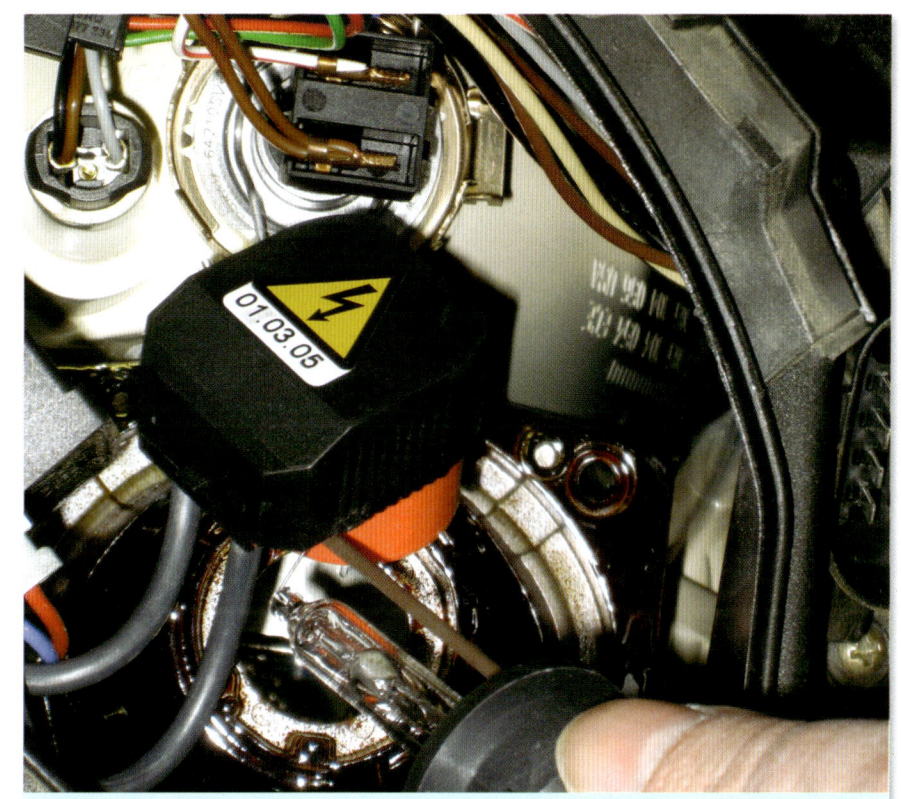

Take care not to touch the bulb glass and note the orientation of the retaining ring in the holder

PORSCHE BOXSTER & CAYMAN

Sidelights – 986
The sidelights (or Parking Lights in the US) are also within the rear of the headlight housing. The holder simply pulls out of the reflector. You can remove the bulb and replace. Note the sidelight for the Litronic bulbs is a small halogen bulb and has offset bayonet pins. Do not try to use a standard 5W bulb as they are not suitable – and will not fit.

Push the holder back into the reflector.

Turn signal (indicator) bulbs
The turn signal bulbs are also in the headlight housing, but are accessed in different ways depending if a 986 or 987.

On the 986 this is underneath the front of the headlight assembly. To remove the bulb, turn the holder counter-clockwise and remove.

The bulb is a bayonet bulb, so ensure it latches in the holder and then replace the holder and turn it clockwise. Notice the thin wires going to the bulb – ensure these are retained flat and clipped under the plastic moulding that is provided for them. If they are left loose they can snag as you replace the headlight assembly and this will damage either the wiring,

Ensure the turn signal leads are clipped into place

The 986 foglights are in the headlamp assemblies

158 Ultimate Owners' Guide

or prevent the headlight latching correctly (which could be disastrous!).

To replace the turn signal bulb on the 987, you access it via a round panel that unscrews on the headlight housing. The bulb is removed by turning the bulb holder counter-clockwise.

Replace the bulb (again a bayonet fit) and replace in the reverse order, remembering to turn the holder clockwise to seat it.

Foglights - 986

In the 986, the foglights are in the headlight assembly, in the 987 and Cayman they are in separate housings in the radiator openings in the bumper cover.

To replace on the 986 there is a round cover in the side of the headlight housing (nearest the centre of the car). Undo this cover and remove. Pull off the plug from the bulb pins, and then unclip the wire retainer and swivel out of the way. The bulb pulls out and can be replaced. Ensure it is correctly seated before replacing the wire clip, and push the connector plug back on to the bulb.

Replace the round cover.

Foglight and parking light – 987

To replace the foglights and parking lights on a 987, loosen the 2 outer screws on the lower face of the clear plastic housing. Note the middle screw is a height adjuster for the fog light and should not be unscrewed.

Pull the loosened light housing down and unlatch the locating cam in the cover projection, continue to remove the housing by unscrewing downwards at an angle.

When removed, access the back and remove the bulb by turning the holder counter-clockwise and pulling out. The bulb is a bayonet-retained bulb. Replace the bulb, and push the holder back in and turn clockwise to fix in place.

To replace the housing, engage the guide pin of the housing on the guide rail, engage the locating cam in the cover projection and press the housing to the rear and push upward until you feel it engage in place. Screw in both the screws.

Foglight and parking light – Cayman

For the Cayman, the procedure is again slightly different. Unclip the light cover – starting on the cover underneath the fog light and pull in the sequence shown in the photo..

To do this you will need to use both hands, and it can take quite a bit of force – you may well wish to take it to a Porsche specialist the first time and ask to watch them do it.

With the cover removed you can undo the 3 screws that hold the foglight in place. Note there is a 4th screw – this is the height adjustment and should not need to be touched – if you are unsure which this is, it lines up with an access hole in the cover you just removed.

Remove the light housing.

To change the fog light, press the retaining tab and remove the plug. Turn the bulb holder clockwise and remove.

PORSCHE BOXSTER & CAYMAN

Replace the bulb then replace the bulb holder and turn anti-clockwise. Replace the plug until you feel it click into place.

To change the parking light, turn the bulb holder counter-clockwise and remove. Replace the defective bulb. Reinsert the bulb holder and turn it clockwise.

Replace the assembly by inserting the bulb housing back into place and replace the 3 screws.

Re-fit the plastic moulding by first inserting into the cut out on the outer side, then press the cover into place at the clips around the sides – starting at the one nearest the centre line of the car. Ensure all the clips are securely back in position.

Side marker lights / Side indicators

The lights on the side of the wings (fenders) can work differently depending on the market in which the car is sold. For instance in the USA, they are side marker lights, and in Europe they are direction indicator lights.

To remove the housing, first using a screwdriver remove the cap behind the housing (in the wheelarch).

Insert the screwdriver in the opening in the wheelarch behind the housing, and disengage the securing spring by pressing with the screwdriver blade. Remove the housing. Remove the bulb holder (a bayonet lock) and you can replace the bulb.

To replace insert the holder into the housing. Insert the housing into the wing at the front first (locate the tabs into the receptor). Clip the back into place engaging the securing spring in place.

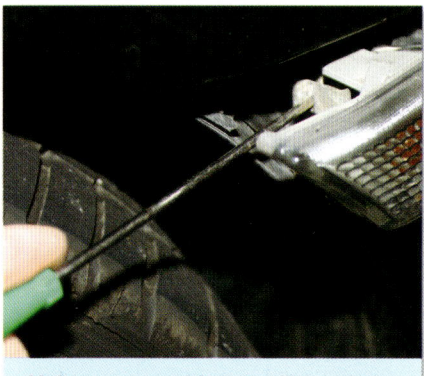

Using a screwdriver to disengage the securing spring for the housing

Replace the cap in the wheel liner.

Rear lights

The rear lights are accessed from within the rear luggage compartment.

First remove the carpet covering the tail lights – there are plastic securing nuts that need to be unscrewed or unclipped to do this.

Press the mounting for the bulb holder upwards (see picture) and carefully remove the bulb holder.

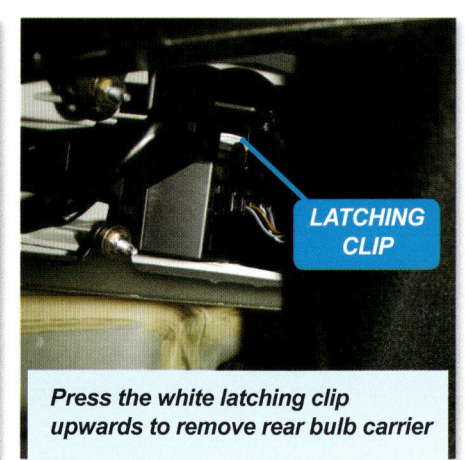

Press the white latching clip upwards to remove rear bulb carrier

160 Ultimate Owners' Guide

All the bulbs are bayonet lock types. Replace the appropriate bulb.

Clip the bulb holder back into place, and replace the carpet.

High level brake light
The 986 uses replaceable bulbs in the high level brake light, the 987 Light Emitting Diodes (LEDs). Unfortunately the LEDs for the 987 are not individually replaceable, so the whole assembly needs to be changed.

To change defective bulbs on the 986:

Open the convertible top so that the convertible top compartment lid is fully open. Remove the ignition key.

Undo the 2 retaining screws and remove the black plastic cover. Be careful here – there is a washer for each screw – and the recess is very deep, it is very easy to lose one of the washers.

With the screws extracted the whole assembly is now removable – you will need access to both sides.

Carefully unclip the six retaining tabs (they are a little fragile and you only need to ease them over the detent). Note there are 3 on the top, and 3 on the bottom of the grey plastic casing. Remove the bulb holder.

Replace the defective bulb(s).

Replace the bulb holder and engage all six securing tabs – make sure you have clicked them all into place, it is easy to think it is done when you hear the tabs click on, but there are often one or two that haven't fully mated.

Replace the black plastic cover and screw the retaining screws back into

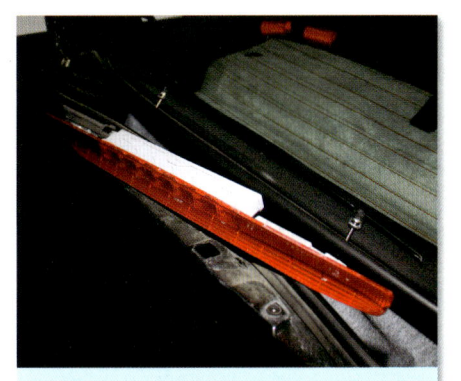

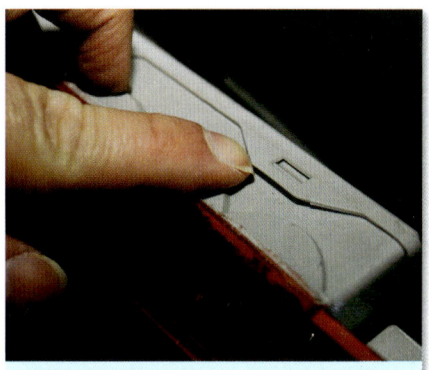

Removing the high level bulb holder on a 986

Carefully unclip the six retaining tabs on the grey plastic casing

place.

Replace ignition key and close the convertible top.

Number (license) plate light
There are two number plate lights at the top of the recess for the rear number plate.

Unscrew both screws to remove the defective light. If there is a rubber covering push this back and remove the defective bulb from between the contact springs.

PORSCHE BOXSTER & CAYMAN

Replace with a new bulb. Reassembly is the reverse of disassembly.

Luggage compartment and Footwell lights

Use a screwdriver to gently press out the light holder from the lining. You might even be able to do this with just a fingernail…

Remove the defective bulb from between the contact springs and replace.

Insert the light back into the cut out one end at a time.

Interior light

Use a screwdriver to gently press out the light holder from the cut out in the lining.

You might find it easier to remove the assembly by unplugging the connector.

Undo the (bayonet lock) bulb holder and remove and replace the bulb. Reattach the assembly to the connector. Replace the light into the cut out one end at a time.

Door guard / Kerb lights (if fitted)

Use a screwdriver to gently press out the light holder from the door carpet.

Pull the bulb holder out of the light housing. Replace the bulb.

Insert the bulb holder back into the light holder and reinsert back into the door carpet.

After replacing any of the bulbs remember to check the operation of all the lights. On the 986 in particular it is easy to disturb the operation of a separate bulb in the process of replacing another.

Headlight adjustment for touring abroad

If you have the Litronic headights option then adjusting them for travel abroad (converting the headlights from left- to right-side driving or the opposite) is one of the easiest things you can do yourself. However the adjustment option is not fitted to cars sold in the USA – I suppose there is no real need. However for those in the United Kingdom who drive in Europe, or Europeans using their Boxster in the UK, the ability to remove the 'dip kick-up' from the low-beam headlights is a real bonus.

This is a really easy job for the owner to carry out, although it is common to see Litronic lights masked up (as normal headlights need to be) because the owner was unwilling to even take a look and see how easy it is. Some even pay Porsche to do the adjustment for them!

You need to remove the headlights as detailed earlier and remove the cover on the rear of the housing as you would when changing bulbs. Inside the housing there is a little metal tab which can be moved between two positions "A" (or sometimes "O") and "T" (these are marked on the metal plate on which the Litronic bulb is mounted). Simply move the tab with your finger from "A" to "T" and that's it!

Reassemble and away you go!

Updating front, rear and side lights

You can update the look of the Pre-2003 986 to the later 2003 MY look by swapping the rear light clusters and the yellow side lights/direction indicators for the new 'clear lens' design (996 side lights are also clear versions and can be used). In the UK it can often be cheaper to use an Official

162 Ultimate Owners' Guide

PORSCHE BOXSTER & CAYMAN

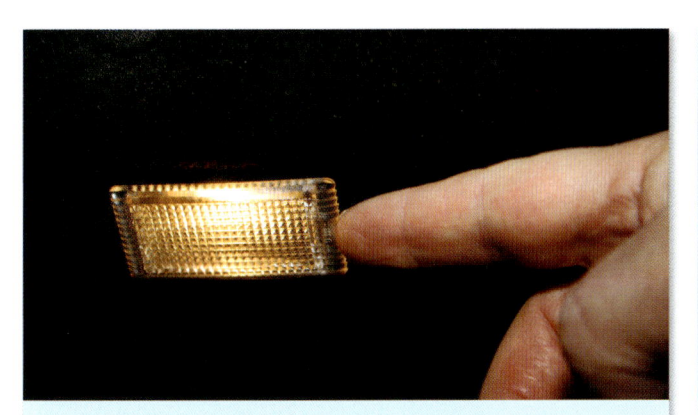

You might be able to ease out the light holder in the front or rear compartments (above), but use a screwdriver to ease out the interior light holder (below)

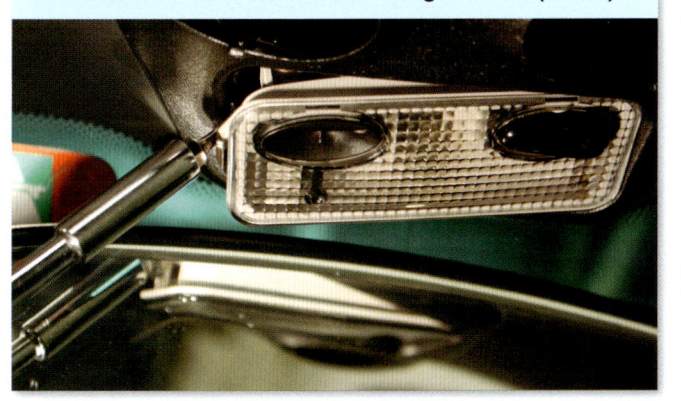

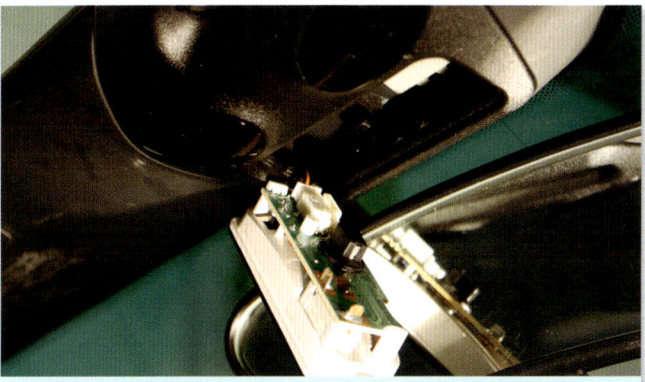

With the holder free, unplug the cable (above) so that you can remove and replace the light bulb easily (below). It is a bayonet fitting

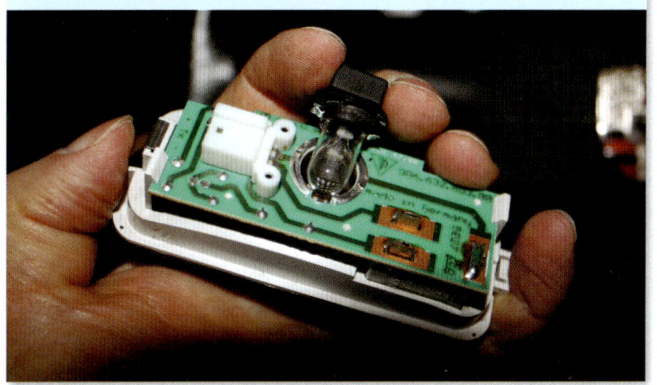

Ultimate Owners' Guide   163

PORSCHE BOXSTER & CAYMAN

It's very easy to change the dipped beam adjustment with this switch (p162)

[TOURING ADJUSTMENT]

Porsche Centre to purchase the parts, some specialist parts suppliers seem to take advantage of people's perception that the official route will be more expensive and actually charge more. In the US the clear lens side lights are available from many specialists.

Only one rear fog light?
Yes, there really is only one rear fog light! Owners who investigate, find there is actually a bulb in the holder, but there is no wire connected to it.

The driver's side is the one that is lit (so left on left hand drive cars, and right on right hand drive cars).

There is only one bulb to ensure at least one brake light is still visible in foggy conditions – and not lost against the bright output of the fog light.

Some owners have connected a wire between the two rear foglights in order to get both working, but due to the safety aspect mentioned here this is not recommended.

Fuses and Relays
The fusebox is located inside the car – down by the driver's feet on the outside wall of the footwell. The fusebox cover has a finger hole to enable easy removal. On 986s, the fusebox cover also frames the switch to manually raise and lower the rear spoiler – useful when cleaning the car. The number of fuses is huge, and unfortunately the circuits covered by any particular fuse location varies from year to year, and from country to country – which is probably the reason that Porsche do not include the list in the Driver's Manual – it would take up pages and be confusing. For the same reason the fuse list has not been detailed in this book. Fortunately, Porsche have included a Fuse Plan appropriate to the year/model/locale of your car on a fold out leaflet clipped to the inside of the fuse cover.

Porsche supply a spare of each fuse rating. However if you have no idea why a fuse has blown in the first place, simply using the spare will likely result in that also failing immediately. NEVER try to compensate for a failing fuse by using one of a higher rating, fuses are there as a cheap way to save your electronics. If the electronics are not protected by the fuse blowing then you will just end up with a much bigger bill.

As the fuses are so tightly packed together you may need to use the extraction tool that Porsche provide (inside the fusebox) to remove the offending item.

Also inside the fusebox is the red terminal for gaining access to the front luggage area when the battery is flat. (See the Emergencies section for further details).

Relays

There are two relay panels, the first is underneath the dash above the fusebox, the other is in the rear luggage compartment, hidden behind the carpet on the left hand side.

Not every relay position is filled on every car. It depends on the specification and the country location.

An example is shown here. This is of a 2001 European model car.

Caution: others may be of different configuration – consult your Porsche Dealer if you have any doubt.

Note that in this picture below of my car, not every position is filled and visibility is extremely limited – the bottom row is mostly hidden behind the carpet.

To access anything you will be laying on your back in the footwell with your feet somewhere in the area of the rollover bars! This is may be why Porsche recommend going to a dealer to have any work done on the relays – it's not the done thing to make owners uncomfortable!

Visibility of the relay panel under the dash is very limited

Ultimate Owners' Guide

PORSCHE BOXSTER & CAYMAN

Relay panel – under dash

From left to right and top to bottom, the relays are as follows (there are 5 units to the first 2 rows, and 6 in each of the remaining three rows).

1	Not Used
2	Not Used
3	Hazard warning flasher
4	Door mirror heater, Rear window demister (hardtop or glass window)
5	1997 – 1998: Telephone speaker relay 1999 – 2001: Not Used
6	Daytime running lights
7	Daytime running lights
8	Headlight washer
9	Terminal XE
10	Horns

11	Bridge plugs:
	    Terminal 15 or 31
	    Terminal 58d

12	Foglights (USA, Japan)
13	Fuel pump
14	Convertible top control module (double width relay)
15	
16	Wiper intermittent control

17	Bridge plugs:
	    Terminal 86S
	    Terminal X, wipers
	    Terminal 15 brake light fuse input

18	A/C and heater system
19	Engine cooling fan left, low speed
20	Engine cooling fan left, high speed
21	Engine cooling fan right, low speed
22	Engine cooling fan right, high speed

23	Bridge plugs:
	    Speedometer terminal A
	    Parking brake signal
	    Terminal 31 electronics ground
	    Terminal 15

24	Bridge plugs:
	    Foglight
	    Terminal 56 right
	    Telephone, cell phone mute
	    Terminal TN

25	Bridge plugs:
	    Terminal 56a
	    Terminal 54 brake lights
	    Parking brake warning
	    Terminal 31d

26	Bridge plugs:
	    Consumer cut-off
	    K2 lead

27	Bridge plugs:
	    Terminal 30
	    Terminal 58

28	Bridge plug: Terminal 31

Relay panel in the rear compartment: 2 rows of 6, plus 2 modules to the front of the main block

1	DME Relay
2	Fuel injectors, Ignition coils, Oxygen sensor heaters
3	Spoiler Extension
4	A/C Compressor
5	Not Used
6	1997, 1999: Not used 1998, 2001: Reversing lights jumper
7	Starter
8	Engine compartment blower
9	Spoiler retraction
10	1997: Spoiler retraction 1998-2001: Secondary air pump
11	1997: Secondary air pump 1998 – 2001: Not Used
12	Not Used
13	Secondary air pump fuse (40A)
14	Oxygen sensor test harness

Ultimate Owners' Guide

PORSCHE BOXSTER & CAYMAN

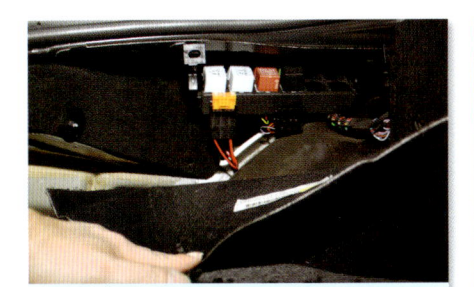

Relay panel in the rear luggage compartment

Modification to enable convertible top operation while moving

There are commercially available modules that allow those with early cars (pre-glass window models) to operate the convertible top while moving. These simply replace the double-wide relay in the relay panel under the dashboard. These modules allow for one-touch operation up and down. However they are quite expensive for what they are. There is an alternative method that can be used. While not as convenient as the

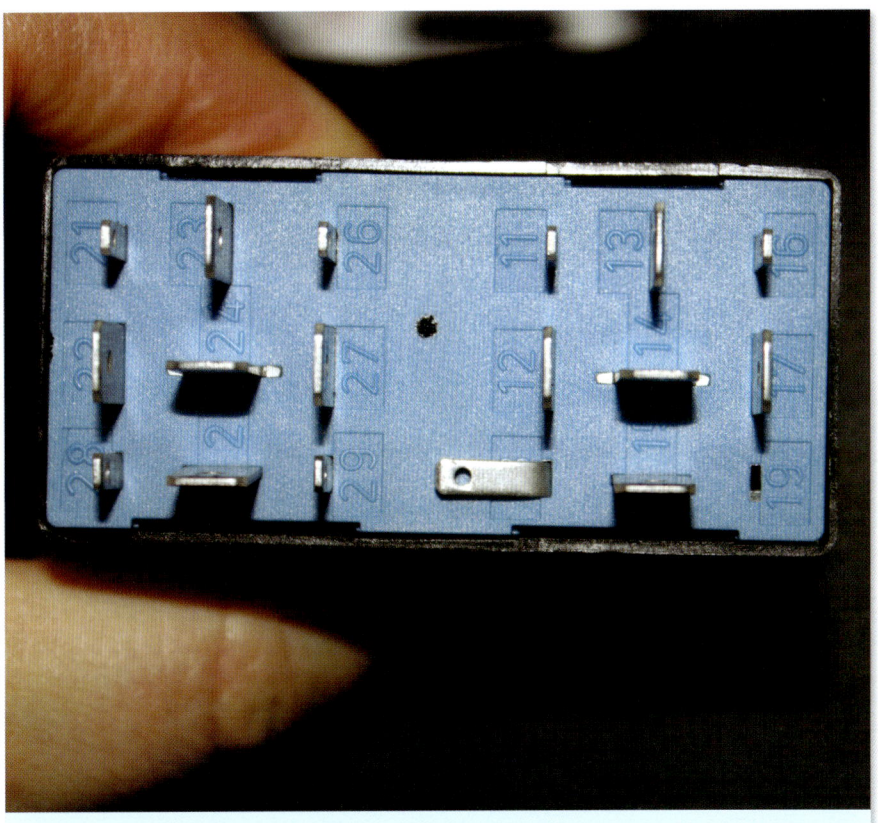

The convertible roof opening relay, with pin 18 bent over

Ultimate Owners' Guide **167**

'one touch' devices, it allows you to raise and lower the convertible top while moving.

Remove the convertible top control module (the double-wide relay under the dash) Bend Pin #18 over into the open area towards the middle of the relay.

Re-install the relay. Test it out. You still have to pull the parking brake on – but only one click (this will not actually operate the parking brake). Press and hold the roof opening button as usual and you can lower or raise the top.

If you try either of these methods to modify the operation of a pre-2003 MY roof in this way I must urge caution – the second method means you have to keep your hand on the switch – so only operate it where safe to do so, and both methods can put extra strain on the roof mechanism. The 2003 MY roof was redesigned and strengthened to enable actuation of the roof up to 30 mph (50km/h) – however the original roof is not designed to do this and I would urge far lower speeds to be used when operating it. You also have no speed-dependant safety cut off – which means that it could be possible to operate the roof at speeds in excess of 30 mph – and if the speed is high enough it could lead to huge damage and possibly an accident. This is a popular modification but you have been warned to use with care!

Alarm/immobiliser system

The Alarm system (if fitted) includes an immobiliser in most markets. This means the car will not start even if you manage to unlock the doors, unless you have the correct key with the transponder that disables the immobiliser.

If a key is lost you can prevent that key from being recognised by the car by having the system reprogrammed at a Porsche Centre (you will need to get the spare keys you purchase programmed to mate them to the system in the same way). However any old 'lost' keys that are disabled in this way will still open the car doors – although the car will not start with them.

"My car has stopped responding to the unlock button"

The above cry for help is very, very common. The reason is normally that the car has not been used in the previous 5 days. After 5 days of inactivity and in order to conserve battery power, the part of the system that 'searches' for the signal from the key's remote lock/unlock is shut down. The system goes into sleep mode, and you need to 'wake it up' in order to get the remote function to work again.

The method used to overcome this varies depending on the model year:
1997 to 2000
Unlock car with key in the doorlock.

Insert key and switch the ignition on to reactivate the keyless entry.

Unfortunately this is difficult to do quickly enough to prevent the alarm being triggered, so in 2001 Porsche enhanced the system:

2001 onwards

Unlock the car with the key in the doorlock (this 'wakes' the car up). Do not open the door.

Press the lock/unlock button on the key to reactivate the keyless entry,

Alarm beeps when locking

When locking the car the alarm should NOT beep. Some mistake the beep as confirming the alarm is set – this is incorrect and a beep indicates that part of the circuit is not complete and is therefore not being monitored. The most common cause of this in 986 models is the centre console storage cubby lid not being closed fully. It is very easy to hit the lock with your elbow while driving and this pops the lid open a little as it unlocks. The alarm senses that this compartment is not closed when you lock the car and so beeps a warning.

There are several areas that will cause an error beep from the alarm:
- The aforementioned console storage box lid not closed fully
- Either front or rear luggage compartments open
- Either door open
- Glovebox (if fitted) not closed fully
- Petrol flap not locked
- Radio sensor

Most of these are fairly self-explanatory. However the radio sensor warrants further discussion.

The factory-fit radio has a small piece of insulation preventing an alarm contact from touching the metal chassis of the radio. If the radio is removed with the alarm set then the contact will touch the radio chassis as the radio is slid out of place and the alarm siren will trigger. If the radio has been replaced, or this insulation is missing, the alarm will beep every time you lock the car to let you know there is a fault (as with all the other conditions listed above). The cure is to put a piece of insulating tape in the appropriate area on the side of the radio.

If the alarm gives two beeps while arming, this indicates there is an error. Any Porsche Centre or good Independent can interrogate the system to find where the fault lies using the system tester.

If you are locking the car but need to disable the interior sensor – for instance if you are leaving someone in the car, or, as I have found, if you need to stop the alarm being triggered by the rear window vibrating on a ferry (the vibrations while the ferry manoeuvres in port make the plastic window vibrate and the interior sensors can trigger the alarm!), just press the lock/alarm button on the remote twice quickly. This disables the internal sensors, and you get a single beep from the alarm to tell you that the sensor is disabled. Ensure that nothing else is open though – as a door or luggage compartment open will not give a separate notification.

TRACKDAY PREPARATION

Trackdays or Drivers' Education events have become incredibly popular over the last few years. They are a great opportunity to take your car out for a good spirited drive without annoying other road users. If you take advantage of having some instruction now and again, this can help you get the most out of your car and enjoy it even more than would be possible (or sensible!) on the road.

There are a few things to think about before taking part in your first trackday. Here are a few to get you started.

Car checks

Before you hit the track there will be a few checks that the organisers will want to make on your car. These include ensuring your battery is securely mounted, that the seat belts are in good condition and that you do not have loose items that can roll around in the car (possibly distracting you, or worse, getting under the pedals). As well as any checks the organisers might make, you will also want to be sure your tyres have enough tread to not only last the track day, but also to get you home legally afterwards as well. Oil and water levels should be normal, brakes not too worn and brake fluid fresh. It can be a surprise to find how quickly fuel gets used, but the organisers normally have a

170 Ultimate Owners' Guide

list of petrol stations either on or off site. Have enough fuel to get you through to the lunch break though – you don't want to miss your turn because you were off getting fuel!

Tyre pressures/nitrogen fill

Tyre pressures can affect the handling of the car on track quite markedly. The stock pressures are a good starting point for track use, but some owners will experiment with them to help overcome understeer or oversteer (push or loose in American terms). I would suggest the trackday beginner just check the pressures are normal (when cold) to begin with.

A good quality pressure gauge is highly recommended for this (see the *Wheels and tyres* chapter). Check the pressures after each session and adjust them as they will increase. At the end of the day you will need to remember to pump your tyres up again, as when normal conditions are resumed and the tyres cool, the pressures will fall markedly.

It is increasingly possible to get a nitrogen fill for your tyres from many tyre fitters. I find this a good idea anyway as the tyres do not heat up so much when the car is driven and pressures stay more stable. In addition nitrogen molecules are larger than the normal air mix and the tyres do not loose pressure so easily.

You still need to check the pressures regularly though and preferably top up with nitrogen or the benefits start to tail off.

As the owner gets more experience they may want to experiment with the tyre pressures. I find slightly higher front pressures suit me (2.2bar or 32 psi) with the stock rear pressures of 2.5bar or 36 psi. Others prefer 2.2bar/32psi F and 2.35bar/34psi R, but this is down to personal taste. I would not recommend varying too much from standard – especially if you are using the different pressures on road. In light of the alleged problems certain car manufacturers in the USA have had with tyre failures when varying pressures from those recommended by the tyre manufacturers, consider very carefully what you intend to do. Do not run at too high or too low a variance from the standard pressures.

Track suspension settings

Experienced owners might want to set their car suspension up to suit regular track work. This can bring more confident handling at the limit but it is an extreme adjustment to make – the tyres will wear unevenly and it is important to inform whoever does your servicing and maintenance if you do set your car to track-based

| | Front || Rear ||
	Standard tolerances	Track day settings (sport)	Standard tolerances	Track day settings (sport)
Toe	+5' +/- 5'	0" 00'	+5' +/- 5'	–0" 05'
Camber	-10' +/- 30'	Maximum negative achievable	-1" 20' +/- 30'	Maximum negative achievable (max –2")

settings. The tyre wear that results will give the impression there is a problem somewhere.

A previous Boxster Register Secretary in the Porsche Club Great Britain, Nic Doczi, recommends the settings in the accompanying table (previous page). Many owners (including myself) have used them subsequently for both road and track use and I've yet to hear of any negative comments.

From experience of these settings, the front tyres will show greater wear on the inside of the tyre tread compared to the outer side. This is because of the increased camber. Most owners however still seem to get the usual wear rate of two sets of rears to one set of fronts in spite of this.

Note that if you have Sports suspension (factory option code 030), it is possible to achieve greater negative camber angles. Increasing this too far will accelerate tyre wear and if you are using the car on the road this wear rate may be more than is acceptable to you.

Correctly torque wheel bolts

This is a reminder to check the wheel bolt torque before your track day - the tightening torque for the wheel bolts is 130Nm (95lbft).

The broomstick test

Or…Rollbar Extensions for broomstick requirement (and are they any good?)

In the USA some drivers ed events require you to pass a 'broomstick test'. This means that drivers of roadster and convertible cars must not have their head (with crash helmet) sticking above the line between the windscreen and the rollbars. When a length of wood, or a broomstick, is placed across the two, the driver's head must be below this implement.

If you are too tall, you cannot run. It's as simple as that. However, there are solutions available that extend the rollbar height to allow you to pass this test. For instance the Brey-Krause roll bar extension bolts to the existing rollbar and allows another couple of inches of headroom. I can't verify it's effectiveness in a roll-over situation – it adds no extra strength to the factory roll bar – but it just allows the broomstick test to be passed.

GT3 Seats and 6-point harness

If trackdays have really bitten you, you might want to investigate the extra control and feel that the GT3-style seat gives you. With the associated 6-point harness you are held in place securely and you will find that you are just using the steering wheel to steer (rather than also to hold on and steady yourself).

The 986 models can use the original Recaro GT3 seats, the 987 and Cayman the 997 GT3 style. These were available to specify when ordering a new car, but not many were actually ordered this way. If you are replacing the original seats with these more track-focused seats, they just bolt in. However you will lose any electrical functions such as height adjustment, heating and position memory. If you have the seatbelt warning alarm you might want to get an old seatbelt buckle from a breaker's yard

PORSCHE BOXSTER & CAYMAN

GT3 bucket seats give a really focused track driving feel to my Boxster S

to disable the 'Bong' alarm while using the 6-point harness. Either that or wear the 3-point belt as well.

You can solve the problem of the warning light on the dash far more easily, with a small piece of electrical tape over the appropriate place in the dashboard!

If you have the space to store spare seats you can swap the GT3 seats in and out fairly quickly and have the comfort of the normal seats day to day, if you think you need to. I fitted GT3 seats to my car 6 months after buying it and they have been in ever since. I've toured all over Europe and have never been uncomfortable. The only problem is that the original Sport seats live in the dining room!

If you are using standard seats there is a device called the CG-Lock that attaches to a normal 3-point seatbelt and locks it in position – without damaging the belt. This can help stop you sliding around and allows greater control as you are not using the wheel to stabilise yourself.

Oil fill and brake fluid change

It's tempting to think "I'll top the oil up as I'm going on track". However, you don't need to do so. As long as the oil is halfway up the dipstick (if fitted) or the appropriate fill level bars on the indicator are lit, that will be fine. You can take a small top-up size bottle of oil with you (the same make and type as you have in the engine), but I bet you won't need it.

Trackdays can however take a fair bit of the useful life out of the oil, so if you do regular days you might want to change the oil more often than the specified service interval.

Similarly trackdays are hard on brake fluid, so heavy track usage means you will want to change the brake fluid more often as well.

Ultimate Owners' Guide   **173**

ACKNOWLEDGEMENTS

I have to acknowledge the people on some websites whose collective knowledge I have been fortunate to have stumbled upon over the years. It all started with Porsche Pete's Boxster Board (www.PPBB.com) where new owners and 'waiters' (those who have placed a deposit and are 'waiting' for their name to come to the top of the list and their car to be built) would discuss the merits and otherwise of their cars.

I was a 'waiter' for some 2 and a half years and I picked up a lot of knowledge from those who were lucky enough to already own Boxsters. As time went on RennTech (www.renntech.org) and the Porsche Club of Great Britain forums (www.porscheclubgbforum.com) have also become great sources of information.

If anything in this book prompts you to look for further information I can highly recommend those sites and of course, joining your local Porsche club – wherever in the world it may be.

In putting this book together I have to thank many people and organisations for their help and assistance:

Porsche Cars Great Britain
Porsche Club Great Britain and its members
Nic Doczi, John Bond, and Nick Pike of the PCGB Boxster Register
Porsche Centre Reading and its staff
Autofarm 1973 Ltd

References
The following were used to verify facts and events:
Porsche: Excellence Was Expected: The Comprehensive History of the Company, Its Cars and Its Racing Heritage by Karl Ludvigsen
Porsche Boxster Story: The Development History by Paul Frère
All performance data is from Porsche Sales Brochures of the appropriate model years

Further Recommended Reading:
Porsche Boxster and Cayman: All Models 1996 to 2007 by Peter Morgan
Porsche Boxster Service Manual: 1997-2004: 2.5 Liter, 2.7 Liter, 3.2 Liter Engines by Robert Bentley

174 Ultimate Owners' Guide

INDEX

Aerokits 68
Air conditioning 143,144
Air conditioning, regassing 145
Alarm, beeps when locking 169
Alarm, doesn't unlock on remote 168
Alarm/immobiliser system 168
Anti-roll/sway bar 115, 116, 120, 121
Automatic gearbox 112
Battery 147
Battery, access when flat 39
Battery conditioner 147
Battery, fixing torques 150
Battery, replacement 149
Battery, top up 149
Black smoke, engine 98
Bodyshell care 44
Bohn, Arno 8
Boxster chop 59, 65
Boxster RS60 Spyder 17
Boxster S 550 Spyder 16
Boxster Sport Editions 20
Brake components, torques 132
Brake disc/rotor diameters 130
Brake disc/rotor replacement 129
Brake light, high level 161
Brake pad and rotor replacement 124
Brake pad replacement 126
Brake pad wear indicators 126, 129

Brake, parking, adjustment 132
Brakes, overview 122
Brakes, rusty discs/rotors 123
Brakes, sizes and caliper colours 123
Brake wear specifications 125
Bumpers, PU 44–46
CAN bus, wiring 147
Car body care 69
Cayman S Design Edition 1 19
Cayman S Design Edition 2 19
Cayman S Sport 20
Centre console 19, 26
Construction & safety 44
Convertible roof, glass window 65
Convertible roof, material care 63
Convertible roof operation 46, 58
Convertible roof, raising manually 61
Convertible roof, retrofit glass window 65, 66
Convertible roof, trouble-shooting 60
Convertible top, while moving 167
Coolant cap replacement 102
Coolant, top-up 101–102
Cooling, engine 143
Cooling, heating & ventilation 143
Corrosion 55
Cylinder failure 97
Dashboard 22

Do-It-Yourself tasks, engine 98
Drain points, clearing 56
Driving lights, removal 51
Droplink, suspension 120, 121
Electrical system overview 147
Emergency wheel, using 142
Engine layout 93
Engine oil and filter change 103–104
Engine overview 92
Engine, top access 98–101
Enhancements and updates 68
Exhaust problems 108
Exhaust tips 110
Expansion tank, coolant 102
Flaps, front wheel, 986 57
Fog and parking light, 987 159
Fog and parking light, Cayman 159
Fog light, only one? 164
Fog lights, 986 159
Front bumper removal 47
Fuel filler 32
Fuses and relays 31, 164
Halogen lights, changing bulbs 156
Headlights 153
Instrument panel 23
Intermediate shaft failure 97
iPod connection 150
Jack, hydraulic, use 34

Jacking the car 41
Jumper cables 40
Lagaay, Harm 9
Larson, Grant 10
Lights, touring adjustment 162, 164
Lights, bulb chart 154
Lights, fitting new bulbs 153
Lights, footwell 162
Lights, Litronic 153, 154
Lights, luggage compartment 162
Lights, rear 160
Lights, side marker 160
Lights, updating 162
Light switch 29
Litronic, changing bulbs 157
Locasil cylinder liners 93, 97
Luggage compartment, front 32
Luggage compartment, rear 33
Lux Pack (UK only) 13
MAF sensor 107
Maintenance schedules 72–91
Manual gearbox 111
Manual gearbox, ratios 112
MOST, fibre-optic network 147
On-Board computer (OBC) 24
P21S polishing soap 69
P21S wheel cleaner 69
PASM 116

Ultimate Owners' Guide   175

PORSCHE BOXSTER & CAYMAN

PCCB 122
PCCB brakes, guide bar 42
PDK 12
PDK gearbox 113
PDK tranmission, ratios 114
Plastic rear screen 58, 62
Plastic rear window, care 58–60, 62–63
Pollen filter 146
Polyrib belt, fitting new 104
Porsche model years 13–15
PSM 122
Radiator access 47
Radiator debris, removal 54
Rear console 29
Rear Main Seal (RMS) 95–97
Relay panel, under dash 166
Relays 165
Short shift gear lever 114
Sidelights (driving lights), 986 158
Sport Chrono 118
Sport suspension, 030 115
Steering 118
Steering wheel adjustment 29
Storage box/luggage net 30
Suspension and steering 115
Suspension, Boxster S 116
Suspension, trouble-shooting 120

Suspension, wheel alignment 118
Tie-rod, steering 121
Tiptronic 12–15
Tiptronic gearbox 112
Tiptronic gearbox, ratios 113
Tool kit 36
Track arm, suspension 120
Trackday, car checks 170
Trackday preparation 170
Trailing/control arm, suspension 120, 121
Transmission overview 111
Turn signals 158
Tyres, age and life 135
Tyres, Bridgestone 139
Tyres, checking for wear 135
Tyres, Continental 139
Tyres, DOT markings 135
Tyres, Dunlop 139
Tyres, Goodyear 139
Tyres, makes 139
Tyres, Michelin 139
Tyres, new 137
Tyres, N ratings 138
Tyres, Pirelli 139
Tyres, Pirelli P Zero 137
Tyres, repairs 136
Tyres, speed ratings 139

Tyres, tread depth 136
TYres, Yokohama 139
Valmet 11
VarioCam Plus valve drive 93
Warning lights 24, 26
Washing the bodywork 69
Wheelarch liners, removal 49
Wheel bolts 141
Wheels and tyres, overview 134
Wheels and tyres, sizes 134
Wheels, options and offsets 139
White smoke, engine 98
Wiedeking, Wendelin, Dr 8
Windstop (Boxster only!) 66

Other practical Porsche titles online at PMM Books
www.pmmbooks.com

Ultimate Owners' Guides
Porsche 911 Carrera 3.2
(ISBN 9781906712020)
Porsche 911 (993)
(ISBN 9781906712068)

Ultimate Buyers' Guides
Porsche Boxster & Cayman
(ISBN 9780954999063)
Porsche 911 The classic models 1964-1989, incl Turbo & 912
(ISBN 9780954999094)
Porsche 944 and 968
(ISBN 9781906712075)
Porsche 911 Carrera, Turbo & RS (964)
(ISBN 9780954999049)
Porsche 911 Carrera, RS & Turbo (993)
(ISBN 9780954999018)
Porsche 911 (996)
(ISBN 9781906712105)
Porsche 911 (997)
(ISBN 9781906712006)